ICE COLD

LEADING FROM THE INSIDE OUT

LEADER

ICE COLD

LEADING FROM THE INSIDE OUT

LEADER

ERROL DOEBLER

WILEY

Published by John Wiley & Sons, Inc., Hoboken, New Jersey.
Published simultaneously in Canada.

For general information on our other products and services or for technical support, please contact our Customer Care Department within the United States at (800) 762-2974, outside the United States at (317) 572-3993 or fax (317) 572-4002.

Wiley also publishes its books in a variety of electronic formats. Some content that appears in print may not be available in electronic formats. For more information about Wiley products, visit our web site at www.wiley.com.

Library of Congress Cataloging-in-Publication Data is Available:

ISBN 9781394239276 (Cloth)
ISBN 9781394239610 (ePDF)
ISBN 9781394239283 (ePub)

Cover Design: Olivier Darbonville
Cover Photo: © 2023 Jessica Jay

SKY10055658_091923

This book is dedicated to those who are on the never-ending search for self-improvement and personal excellence. Regardless of individual circumstance, injury, or trauma, personal and professional excellence will find you as long as you keep looking. Never quit, never give up, never stop searching!

Contents

PART 1

HOW I GOT HERE

Prologue: What I Didn't Know Before

IN THE LATE 1990S, I SUFFERED TWO MAJOR HEAD INJURIES while operating as a Navy SEAL officer which led to my medical discharge. This was a difficult time for me because I loved being a Navy SEAL and had every intention of staying in the SEAL Teams for the duration of what I hoped would be a long military career.

The real shame in this is not that I lost a career I loved. As a result of these head injuries, I was unknowingly suffering from a silent injury called Traumatic Brain Injury, aka TBI, for over twenty years.

For those twenty-plus years, this injury wreaked havoc on my physical, mental, and emotional well-being. Bouts of depression, sleeplessness, and an uneasy relationship with who I was as a human being became my new normal.

In spite of my silent suffering, I managed to live an exciting and fruitful life.

The first edition of this book was written before I knew of my TBI. There was little to no context as to how or why I developed my leadership process and the role the wellness techniques played in my ability to thrive in spite of my injuries.

The severity of my TBI could very easily have placed me in the category of so many veterans today: as of this writing, twenty-two veterans commit suicide each day. But this didn't happen to me.

The process and wellness techniques I created for leadership and personal excellence literally saved my life. They allowed me to find peace in the chaos I was experiencing internally.

What You Will Get from This Book

Part 1 of this book contains stories I have never shared in detail before. They reveal things I did not know about myself and stories I swore never to share. The details of these stories will resonate with you because they represent the struggles we all face.

My hope is that you will be able to feel the pain I describe to you in Part 1—physically, mentally, and emotionally. Why? Because at one point or another, we will all feel physical, mental, and emotional pain. I want you to recognize that you are not alone and that there is a very structured way to move through these challenging times.

Pain and suffering is not a contest. Mine is not worse or better or more harmful than yours. It is simply mine. Our physical, mental, and emotional pain meets us where we are.

I want to provide you with a way to handle your pain, no matter how simple or severe it may be.

I hope my stories will inspire you and show you that there is a way forward, even when you don't know why you are struggling. Sometimes knowing you are not alone is inspiration enough. You are not alone!

As you read this book, I want you to take an honest look at your own life and normalize some of the doubt, insecurity, and fear you face. It is OK to acknowledge these things. It does not make you weak. In fact, because it is so hard to do, acknowledging these parts of yourself only strengthens you. Greatness comes from doing the hard things, and being honest with yourself is a very hard thing.

Part 2 is the first edition of this book, originally titled *The Process, Art, and Science of Leadership*. When I originally wrote it, I had little to no context as to how or why my process worked. Part 1 gives us context. Part 2 gives us the process and the wellness practices to move through personal and professional challenges.

The context I provide in Part 1 along with the details of the process in Part 2 gives even greater credence to my leadership methodology. This book shows the importance of becoming an "Ice Cold Leader."

"We Were Sure You Were Dead"

ONE OF THE COMBAT AREAS OF PROFICIENCY REQUIRED OF a Navy SEAL platoon is Military Operations in an Urban Terrain, or MOUT. This is simply the act of a military unit moving through a city and fighting, usually from house to house. This was typically the type of combat you saw on the news during the War on Terror in Iraq.

One night as my platoon was training, we set up on a house for entry, and I was to be the second man through the door. I would simply go the opposite way the "number one man" went. The number one man's nickname was "Booger." (No secret meaning here. He always seemed to have a hanger disgustingly in view.) In other words, if Booger went through the door and turned right, I would go left. My job was to simply read off of him, go the opposite way, and continue on with the standard house-clearing protocols.

The movements of a proficient military unit making its way through the house are clear and distinct. If a SEAL decides he is going to go to the right, that's it. If it is the wrong move, it will be up to his teammates to make the necessary corrections to ensure a fluid and aggressive flow of movement through the house.

This is why I was surprised when Booger started to go left but then made a sudden jump to the right. It was an unusual display of uncertainty. Despite the speed at which we were moving, I remember clearly thinking to myself, "Huh, I wonder why he did that?" I was about to find out a split second later.

As I stepped to the left through the door's threshold and brought my weapon up to clear my area of the room, I suddenly found myself in a free fall. There was no floor as I entered straight through the door. This is what Booger saw and instinctively jumped away from. (As an aside, night vision goggles were not in play back then. We had flashlights on our weapons that we would turn on as soon as we passed through the threshold of the door. Hence, I couldn't see that there was no floor on the other side of the door until it was too late.)

I always felt bad for Booger—some of the guys gave him a hard time for not warning me. I put a stop to the teasing immediately because it was impossible for Booger to have warned me. We were moving too fast, and I was practically touching him as we went through the door.

I distinctly remember time slowing down as I fell and having a couple of things go through my mind. "Are you shitting me?!" was definitely the first thing. "I wonder how far this fall is going to be?" was next. And finally, "I wonder what is going to be on the floor when I eventually hit?" I was anticipating broken glass, jagged steel, or something awful waiting to make the fall worse.

It turned out to be about a ten-foot fall onto concrete. Not great, but much less bad than I was anticipating. I ended up landing forehead-first. The brim of my helmet shot up upon impact, which exposed my forehead and did not protect me at all. I recently reconnected with one of my teammates, and we had a couple of laughs over the incident. In a flash of seriousness, he relayed to me the sentiment of the platoon after the fall: "We were sure you were dead. The sound of your head hitting the ground was nauseating. We couldn't believe it when you got up."

For better or worse, things were a little different back then when it came to head injuries (and injuries in general). After everyone had some fun looking at the new gash on my skull, we finished up some additional training before I was taken to the local hospital for stitches.

At the hospital, the doctor simply asked what happened and then stitched up my head. We couldn't have been in the hospital for more than an hour. In my medical record, there is a small slip of paper indicating that I was at the hospital. There were no notes from the doctor describing the injury or the treatment. To the best of my recollection, this was at my request.

The next day, I was back at training as if nothing happened. As far as I was concerned, the problem was not my head injury—it was my wrists. After we got back from the hospital, I went to our platoon corpsman's room and told him my wrists were in terrible pain. One light touch of his finger to both wrists gave him all the information he needed. "They're broken, sir. No question about it. What do you want to do?"

Obviously, we weren't going to go back to the hospital because if they cast my wrist, there was a chance I would be removed from the platoon. That was not going to happen. In my mind, my biggest challenge was going to be operating for the next year with broken wrists. So, a couple of ace bandages and some painkillers later, along with some good ole Frogman grit, problem solved. Or at least that's what I thought. As it turns out, my wrists were the least of my problems.

The Aftermath

ABOUT TWO WEEKS AFTER MY FALL, MY PLATOON WAS practicing climbing a caving ladder. We rigged up the ladder to a ship docked in port, jumped in the water, and climbed it. The goal was to get the platoon up the ladder and on board the ship as quickly as possible.

An hour or so into the exercise, as I was treading water waiting for my turn to climb the ladder, I started to feel incredibly sick. The headache and nausea hitting me were like nothing I'd ever experienced. I got up the ladder, and before we went back in the water for another repetition, I told my assistant platoon commander to finish the training. I just needed to sit down for a minute. He gave me an inquisitive look but agreed and went on with the training.

I immediately found a spot to curl up in the fetal position. My head hurt so badly that I literally could not move or speak. I heard my platoon debriefing on the ship about fifteen feet from where I was lying. I heard someone ask where I was. Then, I heard the men gathering up their gear to leave. I was sure I was going to be left there for the night—I was in so much pain I couldn't even yell for someone to help me. Fortunately, one of the men noticed me. The next thing I remember is being in the hospital.

I was able to tell the hospital staff what happened and how I felt. They gave me an IV and some medication to relieve the pain. I stayed in the hospital the rest of the night and vomited the entire time. In the morning, some men from the platoon came to get me from the hospital after I was discharged.

As they helped (carried) me through my apartment complex, I had to stop several times to vomit. Many residents were sitting on their porches having their morning coffee, shaking their heads in disgust at what looked like a stupid young man experiencing the effects of a wild night and too much alcohol. I remember feeling strangely humiliated.

The men from my platoon got me to bed and encouraged me to rest, take the medication the hospital provided, and call them if I needed anything. I remember being relieved it was a Thursday or Friday morning because I would have the weekend to rest and recover.

I took the medication provided, and I immediately knew I was in trouble. I felt even worse. All I could do was lie in bed. I could barely speak, and I certainly wasn't able to get up to get some water.

I had a couple of roommates, but I was gone so often during pre-deployment workup that they never thought anything of the door to my room being closed. They just assumed I was out of town again. I remember thinking to myself that I actually might die in my bed if someone didn't recognize that I was still in there.

Thankfully, my parents knew I was in town. They hadn't heard from me in a few days, which was out of the norm, and called my roommates to check and see if I was in my room. Finally, after about two and a half days of lying in bed with nothing to eat or drink, I was discovered!

I say this lightheartedly, but I honestly remember thinking at some point, "I'm not really going to die in this bed with people walking outside my door all day, am I?" I remember feeling both amused and disturbed at the same time.

I was taken back to the hospital where I was told that the medications were working against each other somehow, and that was the cause of my adverse reaction.

I told the hospital staff that the medication didn't cause the massive head pain I was feeling. They simply replied that the medication certainly didn't help my situation.

Nobody could explain what was happening to me. Nobody asked about or knew about my head injury weeks earlier. It was all a mystery. I spent a week in the hospital and endured three spinal taps. The first two showed an abnormal amount of blood in my spine, and I was told I would be held in the hospital until the spinal tap came back normal.

Thankfully, the third spinal tap came back normal. I was subsequently discharged and sent home. It was the week of Thanksgiving break, so I was given a few days off for convalescent leave and asked if I was ready to get back to work on Monday. Like any good Frogman, my answer was yes.

The headaches never really went away, but I pressed on without complaint.

Getting the Call

DESPITE THE UPS AND DOWNS I EXPERIENCED DURING OUR eighteen-month pre-deployment workup, I was excited to deploy as the platoon commander of a sixteen-man platoon for six months as part of an Amphibious Readiness Group (ARG).

At the time of our deployment in the late 1990s, the United States was in a time of relative peace. It's always a great time to be a SEAL, but as far as work went, pickings were slim. By work, I mean the only work that matters to a Navy SEAL: combat. But we were ready to fight should we get the call. As part of the ARG, we were scheduled to travel to various countries throughout Africa and the Middle East and, should the need arise, meet the call for combat on land or sea in that battle space. The members of the platoon and I had no illusions, though. The likelihood of getting the call to fight was remote at best.

And then, unbelievably, it came. A cargo ship had been identified carrying cargo it was not supposed to be carrying while traveling to a country to which it should not have been traveling. The platoon was tasked with taking down the cargo ship. A Visit, Board, Search, and Seizure operation. VBSS! A classic Navy SEAL operation that the SEAL Teams do better than anyone in the world.

The operation was scheduled to take place forty-eight hours from tasking. This was perfect because it allowed us one day to rehearse, which is not always an available luxury. The platoon could have done the operation without a rehearsal if necessary, which is the very reason we spent eighteen hard months training prior to deployment. Regardless, we were grateful for the extra day to rehearse and plan. However, there was a problem. In the words of the immortal Seinfeld character George Costanza, "The sea was angry that day, my friends—like an old man trying to send back soup in a deli."

All joking aside, the seas were incredibly rough and looked to present a real problem to the operation. Believe me, when a group of Navy SEALs look at the ocean and start to question whether it is possible to conduct an operation, that's saying something. Some of the senior members of the platoon and I looked over the ocean and discussed the potential problems the heavy seas could cause the operation. After some intensive discussion, I felt we had rolled it over enough, "There's only one way to find out. We have the luxury of a rehearsal day, so let's go rehearse."

I made my way up to the bridge of the ship to discuss our launch for rehearsal with the commanding officer of the ship. As I began to relay my recommendations for the rehearsal, he stopped me mid-sentence and said, "You aren't really thinking of launching your boats in this weather, are you?" When I told him that, yes, we were planning on launching to rehearse he replied, "I won't allow it. It's unsafe." So, I replied, "I understand, sir. If the weather holds and is like this tomorrow, will we be authorized to launch for the operation?" "Yes," was his response.

I stood quietly after he confirmed that he would launch the platoon for the operation in the very weather he would not allow us to rehearse in because it was too dangerous. I could literally feel the unspoken conversation we were having. I could feel him comprehend what I was silently saying: "You can't prevent us from rehearsing in the very weather in which you would willingly send us into harm's way."

After a few seconds of this silent exchange, he asked, "How long before your platoon can be ready to launch for rehearsal?"

"The boats and the platoon are ready, sir. The men are just waiting for me to suit up." With that, we were ready to rehearse.

The purpose of a VBSS operation is simple. Board and take control of an enemy ship before anyone on that ship has a chance to respond to your presence. Even in perfect conditions, it is a challenging operation.

The sixteen platoon members would be split between two Rigid Hulled Inflatable Boats (RHIBs). A RHIB is a high-speed, high-buoyancy, extreme-weather craft with the primary mission of Navy SEAL insertion, extraction, and VBSS. They are about thirty-five feet in length and can travel forty-plus knots with a range of approximately 200 nautical miles.

The first (and arguably most important and difficult) portion of the VBSS operation is to secure the caving ladder to the target ship so the SEALs can climb it to board the target ship. A caving ladder is a lightweight, sturdy ladder that can be rolled up. It is about six inches in width, weighs about four pounds, has a breaking strength of over 1,300 pounds, and is generally about thirty-two feet long. Its cables are made of steel, and the rungs are generally lightweight aluminum.

The general concept of this portion of the VBSS operation is to attach one end of the caving ladder to a large grappling hook. Then that large grappling hook is attached to a collapsible pole that can extend to about thirty feet. To get your grappling hook attached to where you want it on the ship you are about to board, you get your biggest, strongest SEAL to heave the pole to the top of the ship to a place where the grappling hook can latch on. A difficult task in perfect conditions.

Once the grappling hook is secured on the target ship, the SEAL operator disconnects the pole with a mighty pull and brings it back onto the RHIB. The caving ladder naturally unfolds when the pole and caving ladder are hoisted to the connection point of the ship. Now, you replace your biggest, strongest SEAL with your smallest, fastest SEAL, who is likely your best climber.

Your best climber acts on faith that his teammate securely hooked the grappling hook to the ship and climbs to the top. Once he is safely on board the target ship, he ensures the grappling hook is safely secured so the rest of the team can safely climb the ladder and begin the takedown of the ship.

This is all done while the RHIBs and target ship are moving at speeds that could be as high as twenty-five knots. To do this successfully, the RHIB must maintain a steady positioning from the target ship. This distance between the RHIB and the target ship can vary, but it needs to be as close as possible, typically a body length or so.

As I said, even under the best conditions, VBSS is a challenging operation to execute. On this rehearsal day, the sea conditions were far from perfect, but we were ready to rehearse so we could ensure a smooth operation the following day. Just as importantly, we were also ready to explain to higher authority why we would not be able to conduct the operation in the current weather state.

As soon as the RHIBs were launched for rehearsal, and we were at sea, I knew we were pushing the envelope of safety, even for Navy SEALs. We would be practicing our boarding on the same ship we were stationed on, which, reportedly, was about the same size as the cargo ship we were to be taking down the following day.

I instructed the RHIB coxswains to conduct several large, looping maneuvers to get a feel for the heavy seas before we approached the target ship. More than anything, I wanted to get a feel for their demeanor. Did they appear overwhelmed and in over their heads, or were they acting methodically and professionally? If they were skittish in the open sea, there was no way I was going to allow them to approach the target ship and attempt to maintain a steady, but close, distance. The coxswains of both RHIBs could not have been more than twenty years old, but thus far, the coxswain on my RHIB was conducting himself with the poise and professionalism expected of a warrior driving SEALs to a target. I radioed over to my chief petty officer on the other RHIB and asked, "How does he look?" His response regarding his coxswain was brief and to the point: "Solid."

Despite the coxswains' solid handling of the RHIBs, my concern was that we were catching too much air. Catching air while trying to maintain station next to the target ship is a recipe for disaster and a "no-go" criterion. I had the coxswains slow down and note the top speed at which we could travel without catching air.

I instructed my RHIB to approach and maintain station until I ordered him to break away. I had to focus my attention on not only the coxswain's demeanor but his skill. As we approached the target ship and began to pull alongside, there was a deafening silence falling over the squad. "Holy shit," I thought to myself, "this is a little scary looking."

As we approached, we were able to see below the water-line of the target ship as it crashed through the waves. In fact, we were able to see far below the water line. This could mean disaster if the RHIB got too close and maneuvered into the huge swell created by the target ship. Could we possibly get sucked into the target ship? I could not even fathom how that would look or how awful it would be if it happened.

I took position next to the coxswain and told him what I wanted from him: "This is dangerous enough, so we are not here to take any unnecessary chances. We are here to see if we can perform the operation in this sea state. If we can't, we can't. It is not a big deal. We go back and wait for another opportunity." My primary purpose here was to ensure the young coxswain took his ego out of what we were doing. I did not want him to think that the fate of the operation was on his shoulders. I wanted to assure him that it was not a big deal if we could not do the operation.

"Can I trust you to get only as close to the ship as you feel safe and not an inch closer?"

"Yes, sir," he replied with the confidence I was looking and hoping for.

The coxswain approached the target ship confidently and quickly found his safe distance. We were close enough to get the caving ladder attached and have the platoon climb and board the target ship. Now the question was how long the coxswain could maintain station. I instructed him to keep station until I told him to break away. This amounted to several minutes on station.

While this was happening, I then asked the operator who would be throwing the caving ladder what he thought. Would he be able to do his job safely in this sea state?

"I think it'll be OK, sir. But I don't know if the pole is long enough to reach where we need to attach the grappling hook." That meant our climb would be at least thirty feet.

"Do you feel comfortable giving it a try?" As with the coxswain, I assured him that it was not a big deal if he did not feel comfortable. It was not a reflection on his abilities. He had to be honest for the good of the entire platoon. He was a seasoned operator and understood what I was saying.

"I can get it up safely," he calmly told me.

"Roger," I responded.

After several minutes of safely holding station, I instructed the coxswain to break away and ordered the other RHIB to take their turn and report back. I could watch the other RHIB from a distance but could not monitor the feeling and vibe on the boat. I had to rely on the chief for that.

The chief of the platoon was excellent, and I trusted him implicitly. He understood the line we were toeing between aggressiveness and safety and would take everything into account as he reported back.

SEAL platoons operate differently in many regards to other combat units. As the leader of the platoon, it was my job not only to make the decisions of safety and aggressiveness that I have described but also to lead from the front. If that means being among the first to launch into a dangerous situation, so be it.

It is not an indictment or judgment on other combat units where the officer places him- or herself somewhere in the middle of the unit. There is merit to that strategy; it just was not the go-to for SEAL platoons. So, the question I was pondering as I watched the second RHIB go through the paces was, "Where is the last place I want to be as we conduct this operation?" Wherever that place was, that was where I needed to be.

In this case, while I would normally be the second or third man up the ladder, the best place to be was off the RHIB and on the ladder. It was uncomfortable, to say the least, waiting for your turn to climb while the RHIB maintained station. I felt it was important to monitor the safety of the evolution and be in a position to make decisions should something go wrong. But, God knows, I wanted to be up that ladder and off the RHIB!

With that in mind, after the chief reported back that his RHIB was good to go, I advised him that we were going to switch the order of the boarding. I would be the last one to leave the RHIB.

I radioed the chief and told him he was the lead boat. Everything else remained the same. "Roger," he replied. Then, the typical SEAL sense of humor kicked in: "Enjoy the long ride," he sarcastically radioed back. I knew it was his way of saying, "Thanks!" And then I gave the order, "Execute, execute, execute."

In any SEAL operation, contingency planning is vital. While we always planned for the actions we needed to execute for success, we also had to act with the realization that things go wrong. Contingency planning involves identifying those things and accounting for them.

Some contingencies are running contingencies, meaning you always account for them. An example is radio communications going down. "What will we do if we lose communications between squads or with higher authority?" The answer will vary from operation to operation, but the contingency is always accounted for.

I had a personal theory around contingencies that I developed from experience and in speaking with some of the senior SEALs who had combat experience from Vietnam. While we were always prepared to execute any contingency plan, you had to take note of how many contingencies you were forced to execute. In other words, operations are hard enough when they go smoothly or without executing contingencies.

Bad things have a way of snowballing. Anything going wrong naturally disrupts the operation. Two things going wrong can disrupt the operation doubly. Three things going wrong … well, you get the point. My personal rule of thumb around contingencies was that the third major contingency you experience during an operation was likely someone getting killed. As a leader, I felt I had to be hyper-conscious of where we stood in an operation if a series of contingencies had to be executed.

For this rehearsal, my contingency radar was on high. If two things went wrong, I was prepared to abort the operation so the third bad thing wouldn't happen—and so no one would get killed.

The trouble started almost immediately when I lost radio communications with the other RHIB. We seamlessly executed our contingency for this possibility, and I made a mental note: "That's one."

We quickly got our radio communications back, and I thought to myself, "Does that still count as a contingency since we got our communications back so quickly? Yes, it does," I concluded.

And then the call came from the chief as they were about to throw up the caving ladder: "The pole just broke. I recommend you take back the lead as we fix the problem." That was enough for me. We had not even started the process of boarding, and already, two major contingencies had to be executed. With the weather the way it was, things were not going to be getting easier. "Abort, Chief. Let's bring it in."

Immediately, the chief radioed back, "The pole is fine, my bad. We're good to keep going."

My mind was racing. Was that two contingencies? One? One and a half? I had to quickly turn to what I would do if this was the actual operation. I made the call: "OK, continue on, Chief."

Within an Inch of My Life, Again

THE AMOUNT OF TIME YOU CAN GET EIGHT SEALS UP A ladder obviously varies depending on sea state, speed of travel, the height of the ladder, etc. Suffice it to say, the speed at which a proficient SEAL platoon can board a ship safely is impressive. Our platoon was proficient, which is why it was extra shocking to see how the sea state and height of the ladder were negatively impacting the platoon's ability to board the ship quickly.

As I observed the second squad climb the ladder, several things were going through my mind. The first thoughts were operational. Was the boarding too slow? Would we be able to maintain the proper stealth and surprise? Was it inherently unsafe given the sea conditions, even though the boarding was happening in what appeared to be a safe manner?

The next thing going through my mind was how much trouble the best in the world at VBSS were having climbing the ladder. It was unbelievable. SEALs will generally self-regulate operational proficiencies. In other words, to conduct a VBSS on a pristine day, our platoon would have at least three men on the ladder at the same time to ensure maximum speed. Today, even though we had thirty feet of ladder on which to operate, the men naturally went no more than two on the ladder at a time. This was naturally safe and intuitive to the operators, which was good. But it slowed us down, which is obviously not so good when we are trying to achieve maximum effect through speed and violence of action.

On the upside, I thought, no one would ever expect to be boarded by a platoon of Navy SEALs in this weather. Even though our speed was suffering, we certainly had surprise on our side. The violence of action would surely occur once the entire platoon was on board and moved to the next phase of the operation.

After the second squad successfully boarded, my RHIB made its approach. While we were experiencing the same struggles climbing the caving ladder as the second squad, the feeling was amplified, once again, by being so close to the target ship. "Get me off this RHIB," I thought on more than one occasion as I waited my turn to climb.

You cannot have a full appreciation for something if you have not done it yourself. The operative word here is "full." Watching the second squad climb the ladder filled me with pride and appreciation for their effort. But until I finally got on the ladder, I had no idea of the magnitude of the challenge. I felt my reasoning was sound for switching the boarding order—until I got on the ladder. I instantly began to question myself.

Once I got on the ladder and felt the difficulty and danger of the climb, I considered whether I would have aborted the rehearsal if I had been one of the first two or three climbers to board the target ship. "I pushed the envelope too far! Fuck! I should have gone first after all!" As these thoughts raced through my head, I immediately began to have counterargument thoughts, the angel and devil on each shoulder representing my internal dialogue.

"No, you didn't push it too far. The men are safely on board. We did it! This is what we are paid for! This is why SEALs hold a special place among all Special Operating Forces! For operations like this!" And then I had to snap myself out of this internal dialogue: "What's done is done! Get up the ladder, finish the op, and then the debrief will allow you to draw the necessary conclusions. One thing at a time. About twenty feet to go!"

The timing to begin climbing was crucial. If you started on the ladder while the boat was at the lowest point of a wave (the trough), you would get slammed in the ass by the RHIB as it rose to the highest point of the wave (the crest) and get knocked off the ladder. The second squad learned that lesson early and passed it along to us immediately: "Get on the ladder at the crest of the wave, and then move your ass!"

Because the crest and trough differentials were so big, the ladder was alternately slack and tense, making it nearly impossible to climb. The ladder did not have the proper tension to climb quickly at the lower half of the ladder. That, combined with the timing needed to get on the ladder from the RHIB, was what led to the slow pace of the group climb. Once the operators got to the halfway or three-quarters mark of the ladder, they could finish the climb strongly.

We designated one SEAL operator from each squad to hold the bottom of the ladder to ensure maximum safety. Before I jumped on the ladder, the SEAL operator holding the ladder and I exchanged a quick, "Hoo-Yah," and off I went.

As expected, the climb became much easier at about the fifteen- to twenty-foot mark. The final ten feet of the thirty-foot climb was standard operating procedure. One of my teammates was waiting at the top of the ladder with an extended hand to pull me over the banister of the ship as quickly as possible. It was a welcome sight!

As I began to reach for his hand, I heard it. SNAP! I knew instantly what happened, and as I began to fall, I blurted out the only thing that came to my mind initially: "Fuck!"

Here's what happened: as the RHIB transitioned from the trough to the crest of a wave, the SEAL operator holding the bottom of the ladder was thrown from his position. When he was thrown, he let go of the ladder, and it hooked on to a cleat (a rope-securing device) on the RHIB at the wave's crest. When the RHIB moved to the trough of the wave, the caving ladder became so taut that it broke from the force, and down I went.

According to some random Google searches I conducted, it takes about one and a half seconds to fall thirty feet. I can tell you from experience that a lot can happen in that second and a half. Even over twenty years later, I am astounded at how many things went through my mind and how clear they still are.

My first thought went straight to leadership. I vividly remember the look of disbelief on my teammate's face as his arm remained outstretched watching me fall. I thought to myself as I looked at him, "Go out like a man. Go out like a leader. Do not thrash or scream or make a show of it. Let the men tell the story of how you remained calm and collected to the very end."

The next thing I thought to myself was, "Good life! I made a lot of mistakes, but they were mistakes of a life lived with passion and enthusiasm. I hope the way I lived puts me in God's hands."

There were some quick flashes of other things that went through my mind that I cannot quite articulate. I do remember, though, thinking about my father. My father and I had a very special relationship, and I remember thinking I was going to miss him terribly. I also remember being afraid for him because I knew my death would hit him very hard. I hoped beyond hope that he would be OK.

Finally, I thought, "Is there any way I can survive this?" I reconciled that there was nothing I could do for myself as I was falling, so I should stay the course and remain calm. I went through the possible scenarios, and none of them looked very good for me.

If you're planning on falling into a RHIB, there's nothing but hazards to land on. The steering console, antennas, radars, weapons mounts—all things that would certainly impale me should I land in the boat. But landing in the boat is not what I anticipated would happen.

What I was sure was going to happen was I was going to fall in between the RHIB and the target ship. If this happened, there was going to be only one outcome: I was going to get sucked underneath the massive Navy warship, into its huge propeller screws, and chopped up into a fine fish food. With that realization, I resigned myself to one outcome: "I hope it happens fast!"

And then, BAM! I hit the boat.

In times of chaos and stress, you go to what you know. You go to what you have programmed yourself to do automatically, be it consciously or unconsciously. The phrase, "You fight like you train," never rang truer for me than after I realized I was still alive.

It turns out I landed on the one part of the boat that would allow for my survival: the cover over the engine was the only flat and unobstructed surface area on the boat. Miraculously, this is where I landed. The only downside was that my left elbow hung over the side of the cover when I landed, so the momentum of the fall snapped my elbow.

As I bounced about ten feet in the air off the boat, I suddenly realized I was still alive and went immediately and unconsciously into action mode. I noticed that my left arm was dangling uselessly as I was suspended in the air. "If you land in the water, don't try to swim. Instead, focus all your energy on pulling your CO_2 cartridge on your life vest to keep you afloat. You won't be able to swim," I ordered myself.

That was my plan should I land in the water with the RHIB between me and the target ship. If, however, I landed in between the RHIB and the target ship, my fate was still likely being sucked into the propeller. I resolved, however, to die trying to find and pull my CO_2 cartridge, regardless of which side of the RHIB I landed on.

As I descended and awaited the moment of truth, a miracle happened. I landed safely on my ass in between two objects on the RHIB that would have either further injured me had I landed on them or directed me over the side of the RHIB and into the ocean. I could not believe it. I was alive! Left on the boat were the coxswain, his partner, my SEAL teammate who was holding the ladder, and me. "Hahaha! Holy fucking shit!" I exclaimed, to no response from anyone on the boat.

The three young men remaining on the RHIB with me barely had sixty years between them and appeared to be in a bit of shock at what they had just witnessed (rightfully so). "Break away and call the command ship. Advise them I am alive. Tell them we are ready to be brought on board and are coming around to station now," I ordered. The coxswain, to his credit, never moved from station until I ordered him to at that moment. His ability to keep the RHIB on station no doubt saved my life.

All seemed pretty good, except—shit! I noticed blood soaking my flight suit from my left elbow. "Advise them I have a broken left arm at the elbow, but otherwise, I'm fine."

Spurting blood is never a good sign. It quickly became apparent it was not spurting blood, just a steady drip, but I still needed to stop the bleeding fast. "Get me a bandage," I called over to my teammate.

"Bandage" was barely out of my mouth when the bandage hit me in the head. "Well, I guess I'm going to do this myself," I thought. My teammate quickly realized what he had done and came over to offer assistance. I told him I was OK and was going to wrap it myself. I knew it was going to hurt and felt I might punch the person who tried to wrap it for me in the face. Since I was able, I thought it best to administer my own aid for the benefit of everyone involved.

As the boat was lifted out of the water and on to the deck, I was met by the ship's corpsman and a stretcher. "I can walk," I told him. As we were walking to his office so he and his team could administer aid to my injuries, I felt the eyes of everyone on deck on me. I felt like I needed to do or say something. I'm not sure why I felt this way. I think walking away from this fall should have been enough.

Instead, though, I bellowed, "This is why we rehearse!" To this day, I have no idea what message I was trying to convey or to whom. But that is what I went with. In hindsight, it would have been way cooler if I had just kept my mouth shut.

The corpsman and his team were also extremely young, and I found myself making jokes to lighten the mood. My behavior served to lighten the mood a little too much because there was very little urgency to get me the drugs I knew I would desperately need at any moment. "Doc, I think I've got about two minutes before the shock wears off, and I start feeling some real pain. Can we hurry up with the drugs, please?"

With that, drugs were administered, and I was moved to the helicopter that was standing by to transport me to the hospital ship that was part of the battle group.

Upon arrival at the hospital ship, there seemed to be a little more chaos than I expected as I was surrounded by what seemed like half a dozen senior officers giving orders to nobody in particular. Mind you, I was in the fog of a healthy morphine injection. However, something stood out amid the chaos of voices: "If I'm not needed here, I'm heading out," I heard someone calmly say.

"Everybody stop!" I yelled to the shock of everyone present. After all, I was only a lieutenant—a much lower rank than those shouting orders. "Who just said that?" I inquired.

"I did, why?" came the response.

"Because I'd like you to stay. You're the only one making sense," I replied.

"Well, you heard him, Gentlemen. I'll take it from here." It turns out it was the anesthesiologist, the most important person to be there. And with that, all non-essential personnel left the area grudgingly. I say grudgingly because nobody at that rank likes to acknowledge they are non-essential.

"Thanks, Doc," I said. "Things seemed to be getting a little out of hand, huh?" Even though I was beginning to fade from consciousness, I'll never forget the way the doctor looked at me, looked around at those remaining, looked back at me, and asked, "You're the SEAL who just fell from the ladder, right?"

"That's me," I responded with less than proper military bearing.

"Thirty feet from the ladder into the RHIB, right?" he confirmed.

"Thirty feet sounds about right," I answered.

"How much morphine does this man have in him?" he asked with a touch of confusion and concern. I recognized the voice of the ship's corpsman answering the doc's question. His actual answer meant nothing to me, but it clearly meant something to the doctor.

"Well, that explains it. Great, that's enough morphine to knock down a horse." I guess my demeanor, in the doctor's mind, was not that of someone who had suffered an injury of the magnitude I had just experienced.

He quickly went on to explain that it looked like my arm had dislocated at the elbow, and they needed to pull it back in place before they began operating. I recalled my arm dangling aimlessly after I hit the RHIB and bounced into the air.

"That sounds painful, sir. Any chance I can get another hit of painkiller before you do that?" I asked.

"Young man, feeling pain is not going to be your issue. Waking up from all the morphine in your system is going to be your issue," he calmly explained.

I'll never forget my thought right before I faded into unconsciousness: "Wouldn't that be ironic—dying from an overdose of painkiller."

Humiliation, Shame, and Silence

MONTHS LATER, I STOOD BEFORE THE MEDICAL REVIEW board convened to assess my injuries from the series of falls while I was in the SEAL Teams and determine what, if any, financial compensation I should receive as a result of my injuries.

"Lieutenant. Doebler, I have to say, we were very curious to see you, a Navy SEAL officer, today. We are obviously aware of what happened to you and the recommendation that you be medically discharged from the United States Navy. However, it's hard to make a judgment because, if I can be honest, you look fine."

This was my first experience with what we now understand to be invisible injuries. And it didn't get much better after this opening salvo.

Another board member chimed in: "Usually, it is easy to assess damages because the people who come in here are usually missing a limb or a hand or a finger—something that shows they have been injured. You look healthy and in great condition."

A wave of emotions came over me. I felt angry that I was being put in a position to defend myself. "You asked me here! I'm being punished because I continued to take care of myself after I was injured?!" I wanted to scream. Then this thought raged through my mind as I stood there: "Do they think I'm here to beg for money?!"

I'm pretty sure a couple of other board members spoke, but I have no idea what they said. I was in a fog. I had no idea what to say or how to respond. In typical SEAL fashion, I decided to go on the offensive. I was ready to tell the board, with all due respect, that I didn't want anything from them. If they thought nothing was wrong with me, then we should save ourselves a lot of time and end this ridiculous review board because I wasn't going to stand there and be insulted!

So, I steadied myself, took a deep breath … and cried.

That is when the shame kicked in. Here I was, an officer in the world's most elite fighting force, a leader of men, crying in front of total strangers. I felt shame that this was how I was representing the organization that meant everything to me.

"Leave!!" I shouted to myself. "Don't do any more harm to the reputation of the SEAL Teams."

Instead, I meekly responded, "I'm not here to ask for money. I'm here because I was ordered to be here. However, I just have a feeling that my injuries are not healed, and I may need some medical attention down the line. I just hope that I won't be forced to pay for this out of my pocket."

I was asked to elaborate.

I had lost some use of my hand due to my ulnar nerve being severed from one of the falls. This is what I focused on. I told them that no one could assess whether I would recover full use of my hand. What's more, I added, there was still a terrible pain in my wrist when I moved my hand.

And then, ever more meekly, I said, "And I just can't stop these headaches. They just never seem to stop."

I can't remember much after that, other than the fact that I felt humiliated. I left that meeting feeling more insignificant than I had ever felt.

The shame of my injuries didn't end with the board review.

There was very little discussion, if any, around the effect of my head injuries. As time went on, I focused on managing the headaches, what triggered them, and trying to "see them coming" so I could rush to bed before they got too bad.

On several occasions while driving, I had to pull over on the side of the road or highway and sleep because my vision became so blurred, and the pain was overwhelming.

Finally, the pain in my wrist became so bad I went to the military hospital in Bethesda, MD. I had to force my way in for an appointment. The War on Terror was underway, and the priority, rightfully so, went to active-duty members.

The humiliation and shame continued as "forcing" my way in for an appointment turned into begging for an appointment. Finally, I was given an X-ray of my wrist and scheduled for surgery. The X-ray revealed two bones floating around my wrist which were the obvious cause of my pain.

As I was prepped for surgery, the doctor came over to do her standard, pre-surgery check-in. I was ready to thank her for doing the surgery, and I wanted to ask her about my headaches. Any thought of conversation ended immediately upon the doctor's comment to me: "We have people serving in here who need our help."

The message to me was clear: "You don't belong here."

Once again, I found myself stunned and ashamed. My response was even meeker than the one at my medical review board: "I'm sorry." And then, more under my breath than an actual audible sentence, I added, "I served."

After completing the surgery, the doctor came over with the two large pieces of bone she removed from my wrist floating in a jar. She asked me, giddily, if I wanted them as a souvenir of sorts.

"No, thank you," I said. And I left.

I vowed then and there that I would never speak of my injuries again—especially the headaches.

The shame and humiliation of my invisible injuries were complete.

By and large, I held true to my pledge of never speaking of my injuries for the better part of twenty years. Friends and colleagues periodically asked about what happened to me and why I left the SEAL Teams. Sparingly, and with little to no detail, I shared the stories of my injuries. But I never discussed the effects the injuries had on me. I recall a couple of instances explaining to people that I probably could have stayed in the Navy and waited out my arm injury to see if I would get full use of my hand back. I don't know this to be true, but I said it anyway. I always followed up with, "But the headaches … they just come on so fast. My fear is that I would be in the field operating, and a headache would come on, and I would compromise the operation because, well, they are debilitating …" and I would trail off.

I know I only shared those thoughts a handful of times because I remember the blank stares of the people with whom I shared this information. In hindsight, I'm sure they were looking at me like that because they simply didn't know what to say or how to respond. But at the time, it was not how I interpreted it. I felt judged.

These memories are so vivid to me. Every time I shared my feelings around my fear of operating because of the headaches, my memory immediately flashed to a former teammate at SEAL Team Four. This teammate fought in the invasion of Panama in 1989 (Operation Just Cause) and was wounded. Half of his calf was shot off, but he remained operational years after his injury.

Each time I shared my fear, I would remember my former teammate's mangled calf and tell myself, "He stayed. I left. What a pussy I am."

Again and again, I vowed to myself to never express my true feelings around my head injuries.

For the Next Twenty Years ...

NOW IS ABOUT THE TIME WHEN I SHOULD SHARE STORIES with you about how these head injuries affected me physically, mentally, and emotionally. The problem is I have trouble remembering a lot of specifics. I do, however, remember the feeling of my struggles.

Emotionally, I began to feel like I wasn't good enough for anything. I didn't feel like I was worthy of a solid romantic relationship with anyone. I'm not sure how many relationships I sabotaged, but I know there were more than a few.

I didn't feel like I measured up in social circles. This person or that person was clearly better than me personally and professionally. Not feeling like I measured up to anyone, anywhere tore me up inside.

Because I didn't feel like I measured up, I constantly felt like I was being slighted by people. I would stew over a perceived slight. I felt like people were intentionally disrespecting me. I would carry that anger and shame with me until I could, in some way, shape, or form, return the favor to the "guilty" party.

To this day, I don't know how many times I was actually slighted, but my guess is not many. If I chose to confront the person directly, I would let them know in no uncertain terms that any more slights or disrespect would be conducted at their peril.

As I think back on these instances, I can vividly recall the look of confusion on the person's face. I'm sure the confusion had something to do with the fact that they had no idea what I was talking about.

My form of retribution to these unsuspecting individuals never made me feel better. In fact, they made me feel ashamed of myself, which led to a deeper sense of self-loathing. This led to serious bouts of depression that would last for days at a time.

In spite of myself, I found success in many areas of my life. This never made me feel good, though. I never found any success worthy of celebration or acknowledgment. I always felt that my successes must have been handed to me or that anyone could have done what I did. I would love to think this mindset was due to humility. Perhaps some of it was. But I simply felt unworthy of any success or praise.

I feel like there was always some legitimate reason why I felt sad, mad, or happy during this difficult time. The problem was, though, that any emotion I felt was exhibited to the maximum extent.

I met the slightest annoyance with the full force of my anger. These outbursts weren't extended anger, but they were short, furious exhibitions of anger. And then, of course, I would feel terrible about myself after the emotional hurricane subsided.

We are all allowed to be sad. But even the smallest, minorly sad event would take me to a dark place. Even happiness was taken to the extreme. Extreme exuberance over the smallest thing is not always the proper response.

In short, I had no control over the extent to which I would express my emotions. I began to get a reputation as a loose cannon. In some ways, I suppose I was, but I never believed that was truly my character. It bothered me to no end that people would sometimes look at me that way.

Then the cycle of self-loathing would begin again.

Here is a small example.

When I was attached to the 75th Ranger Regiment as an FBI Special Agent in 2010 for combat operations in Afghanistan, I was awarded The Shield of Bravery for my actions in combat. It is the FBI's second-highest award for valor.

When I was notified about the award, I was confused. I called the appropriate office to inquire about it and tell them there was a mistake. I informed them that I would not accept an award that I did not earn. The lady with whom I was speaking was confused, but she informed me that it was not a mistake. I had earned the award.

I was later informed that there was to be a formal awards assembly. I RSVP'd "Not attending." One of the men who also won the award in Afghanistan called me when he heard I wasn't attending the ceremony. He asked me why, and I told him I had a prior commitment. He told me I had to come. If I didn't, they probably wouldn't formally recognize me at the ceremony, and that would be a shame.

I didn't relent, and I was not formally recognized at the ceremony. I didn't think I deserved the award in the first place.

The people with whom I came into contact over the twenty years since my injuries will have trouble believing this is how I was feeling. They would probably say I was passionate—the opposite of what I've just described.

How can this be? How could I have felt these ways but achieved a large degree of success both personally and professionally? Why will people be surprised that I struggled so mightily?

This is where my process was born.

CHAPTER 7

Fast Forward to 2020

B Y THIS TIME, I HAD STARTED MY LEADERSHIP CONSULTING firm and wrote and published the first edition of this book. I appeared on many podcasts to promote my book and company. One of the podcasts I appeared on was former Navy SEAL Mark Divine's "Unbeatable Mind."

I felt a great deal of trepidation around this podcast appearance because I could count on one hand the number of Navy SEALs I had spoken to in the twenty-plus years since I left the Navy. Because of the shame I felt after all the years, because of how I left the SEAL Teams, I considered canceling the appearance. My wife convinced me not to cancel.

There is a reason Mark Divine is so successful and has such a loyal following. It is because he is an awesome human being. I'm not sure where I would be had I chickened out and not appeared on his podcast because he may very well have changed the trajectory of my life.

About halfway through recording with Mark, I was telling the stories that led to my injuries. I had never gone into that amount of detail about my injuries before. It was ironic that the person I finally shared with was the type of person I was so afraid would judge me the harshest: a Navy SEAL. I could not have been more wrong.

At one point, he interjected and commented that perhaps my series of bad decisions and downward spiral when I left the SEAL Teams were all a result of my head injuries. Mark mentioned Traumatic Brain Injury and the effects it has both short-term and long-term.

I awkwardly thanked him for that acknowledgment and moved on with my story. After the podcast was over, I told my wife about the interview, then said, "But you know, Mark said something really interesting. He said my string of bad decisions toward the end of my SEAL career was probably a result of the head injuries and that I should cut myself some slack. He mentioned TBI."

My wife's response was simple and dripping with loving sarcasm: "Ya' think!?!?"

During the podcast, I acted like I knew what Mark was talking about. But in all honesty, I had barely any knowledge of TBI, let alone what it can do to a person. This was the first time someone indicated that perhaps there were circumstances beyond my control that led me to spiral out of control and act irrationally on my emotions.

I didn't know what to do with this information, so I tucked it away for reflection.

One evening, not long after appearing on Mark Divine's podcast, my wife and I went to a cocktail party. I met a doctor there who specialized in treating TBI with natural protocols; in other words, he treated without pharmaceuticals. The doctor focused his practice on helping veterans and professional athletes. Without thinking too much about it, and in the spirit of making conversation, I shared my history of serious head injuries, especially during my time in the SEAL Teams.

"So what happened?" the doctor asked me.

"I just told you what happened," I responded with a bit of confusion.

"No, what happened to you after the injuries? What were the effects?" he clarified.

I'm certain that my experience with Mark Divine helped me break the fear of talking about my head injuries, or at least how I got them. But this guy was asking me a deeper question. The answer was truly something I never talked about. I thought to myself, "If I can't talk to a guy who is dedicating his life to helping people like me, then who am I? What kind of selfish coward am I?"

"Well," I began, "I haven't had a full night's sleep for as long as I can remember. Sometimes I get really sad, and it takes several days for me to snap out of it. I have trouble controlling my emotions. Sometimes I get really angry for something silly. Sometimes I don't get angry when I should. Sometimes I even take my happiness overboard, if that makes sense."

"It does," the doctor responded.

"But most of all, I just feel angst all the time. I feel like there is a volcano bubbling up inside me that never quite lets me relax. I'm constantly on edge about what I'm doing and thinking all the time. I just get so tired."

He nodded in understanding.

After I was done, I expressed my true gratitude for the doctor's efforts to help our service members and others who are suffering and need a natural alternative to the predictably bad, ineffective, and ultimately destructive path of pharmaceutical medication to help the effects of TBI.

And that was it. The evening was coming to an end, and I thoroughly enjoyed speaking to the doctor. I did not anticipate seeing him again anytime soon. As we were saying goodnight, he asked if I would come into his office for a brain scan.

I remember thinking that this must be the doctor version of, "Let's meet for coffee sometime." It's a nice gesture after you meet someone, but no one ever really follows up on it. I told him I'd be happy to come in.

The next day, I received a call from his office to set up a brain scan. I agreed to go in.

The brain scan I was to undergo was a "WAVi" scan, which measures, among other things, the energy in your brain. I came to find out that CT scans and MRIs cannot detect brain injuries.

I was scheduled to have the WAVi brain scan on a Monday. The Saturday night prior, my wife and I were relaxing, discussing our anticipation of the scan. What would the scan tell us? Was it possible Mark Divine was right? Was a TBI the reason I struggled so mightily to properly process my emotions which led to my unwanted or destructive behavior on so many occasions? Was this scan going to give me answers? Yes, one way or another, it was going to give me answers.

Then a thought came to me that scared me to death: What happens if the WAVi scan shows there is no damage to my brain? What if there is no good reason for my behavioral struggles over the last two decades? What if I'm just ... a jerk?

"I'm having second thoughts about going in for the scan," I told my wife out of the blue.

"What? Why?" was all she could say in reply.

I proceeded to rattle off a series of ridiculous reasons as to why I should not get the brain scan after all. I concluded with, "What difference does it make at this point?"

My wife was speechless but was used to this type of unpredictable reaction from me. Her response was concise and to the point: "Well, for one thing, the life insurance company raised your rates by a factor of eight because they said brain injuries can cause early onset dementia, Alzheimer's, and early death. Your three children and I would like to have you around if that's OK with you."

I conceded the point and agreed to go. But I was scared— not so much of what the brain scan might show but of the exposure of my own fallibility as a human being.

Long-Awaited Answers

A S I COMPLETED THE SURPRISINGLY SHORT AND UNOB-trusive WAVi scan, the doctor printed out the results.

"Do you see these two wavelengths operating in harmony and unison?" The doctor asked me. "This is the energy of your heart and brain waves acting in perfect sync. This is common for people who are committed to a life of mindfulness, meditation, and happiness."

"OK," I responded.

"Do you see this area of your brain that is red? This shows that your brain is in a high alpha state." The doctor went on to explain that the alpha state is the most desirable state for your brain to be in. It means that I am calm and at ease but also focused and aware of what is happening around me.

Calm and at ease? Heart and brain in perfect harmony?

It sounded good, but it was difficult for me to believe because of the inherent angst I constantly felt bubbling below the surface.

"OK," I thought. "And what? This is nice to hear but ultimately doesn't mean much to me." And then he hit me with the final piece of information.

"Do you see this area of blue around your brain?" he asked.

"Yes," I replied. It was hard to miss because there was a substantial amount of blue.

"This is the area of your brain that controls how you process emotions. The blue indicates that this part of your brain is essentially inactive. It's dormant. This is an indication of someone who suffers from severe TBI," the doctor informed me.

"OK," I replied again.

"You don't get it, do you?"

"No, I get it," I replied.

"No, I don't think you do. Your heart and brain waves are in perfect sync. Your brain is in the perfect alpha state. These conditions are completely inconsistent with your inability to process emotions based on your TBI," he explained.

My mind was racing. I was stunned and speechless. He was right. I hadn't gotten it. The enormity of the situation started to overtake me.

The doctor was curious about the inconsistencies of the scan: "Tell me about your leadership process you teach. How did you develop it? How long did it take to develop?"

I explained that the leadership process begins with emotional awareness, understanding the intuitive reaction based on the emotion, establishing a desired behavior, making a plan to execute the desired behavior, and finally having the understanding that this process served to rewire the brain and that we all need to leave room in our lives for some grace, should we fall off track.

In the end, I explained how being aware of your emotions leads to better decision-making. Better decision-making leads to a better, less stressful life. But imagine working so hard to create a behavior that never gets hardwired in your brain. Then imagine knowing that if you don't continue the behavior, you will likely send your life into a downward spiral you may not recover from.

This was my life. All day, every day, I was either thinking about my emotions and how I should act on them or reflecting on how I acted without considering my emotions and then trying to make up for the poor decisions I made. I did this unceasingly without the benefit of my hard work becoming second nature. The part of my brain that would benefit from this work wasn't working.

It was like Groundhog Day, except it worked by the hour. Sometimes by the minute. So, it was Groundhog Hour.

"That sounds exhausting," the doctor exclaimed.

"It is," I responded.

I continued this process, despite how exhausting it was, because I knew the alternative was unacceptable. I had faith that, someday, my work would form a habit that would not drain my emotional and physical energy by the hour.

As he contemplated the leadership/problem-solving process I developed, he continued, "OK, tell me about these ice baths. What role do they play?"

I explained I was a certified instructor in the Wim Hof Method, a wellness practice that combines a unique breathing technique, cold exposure, and mindset.

"I use the Wim Hof Method in a couple of different ways," I explained. "First and foremost, it is a science-based practice that has shown that individuals can exert conscious control over their autonomic nervous system and innate immune system. In short, it strengthens your immune system and dampens the inflammatory response caused by disease. It also resets the nervous system by removing stress-induced inflammation from the body."

The doctor said he had heard of the method but was not fully aware of the scientific studies behind it.

"Being in an ice bath also teaches us how to deal with stress. It's basically an induced panic attack. When I practice recognizing the symptoms of panic or stress, like what is created in an ice bath, and then learn to breathe properly and relax while in a tub full of ice, I am then able to do the same for myself during my day. Essentially, it's hard for stress to get the better of me because I practice relaxing in an ice bath."

The doctor was nodding in agreement.

"In short," I continued, "I use the breathing and cold exposure techniques to clear the inflammation in my body caused by stress and reset my nervous system. That way, I can focus on practicing my leadership technique that allows me to make good, conscious decisions.

"If my nervous system is reset and the inflammation in my body cleared, I'm not suffering the ill effects of inflammation. Inflammation, as we now know, is the major driver for just about every life-threatening disease we know of today."

The doctor continued to nod in understanding.

"If I'm not worried about the ill effects of inflammation and a shot nervous system, I can think about making good decisions," I told him.

After a moment of contemplation, the doctor weighed in: "Well, that explains it," he told me. "You've basically saved your own life."

I looked at him with some confusion.

"Errol, your TBI is so severe that, at best, these injuries should have led you to a very dark place. At worst, you should be a statistic. You are neither. You are a highly functioning individual who has fought through the effects of a brain injury you did not even know you had."

The statistic the doctor was referring to is that twenty-two veterans a day commit suicide because of injuries like mine that lead them to very dark places of hopelessness. This was a jolting commentary because I knew of the dark places to which he was referring. I knew them all too well, but I somehow managed to avoid getting entirely and hopelessly sucked into them.

I knew the reason I avoided getting immersed in these dark places is that, after I left the SEAL Teams, I began an intensive process of reflection to understand why I made some of the reckless decisions I was prone to making and, on the other end of the spectrum, why I was able to achieve such success in the most challenging of circumstances.

This reflection made clear to me that emotions were at the root of every action I took, both good and bad. The difference was, however, that when I was aware of and acknowledged my emotions, I was in control of the action the emotion inspired.

When I was not aware of the emotion and failed to consciously acknowledge it, I was not in control of the action the emotion inspired.

Further reflection on this fact led to an obvious observation. I was able to link my good decisions with the ability to be aware of and recognize the emotion I was feeling before I acted. Essentially, I was able to make a conscious decision on how I should act despite my emotion. Predictably, conscious decisions lead to good outcomes, regardless of the emotion that preceded the action.

"You've taken yourself as far as you can, Errol," the doctor told me. "Now let me take you the rest of the way toward recovery."

Once again, I was stunned. Recovery?!

What the doctor was talking about was a non-pharmaceutical process that didn't simply mask the symptoms created by a brain injury, but healed the brain. A more traditional pharmaceutical process had proved ineffective for those veterans that eventually committed suicide.

It was a strange moment of unworthiness I was experiencing. I strangely felt that I was not worthy of a treatment that would heal me and change my life for the better. I became very emotional.

"I appreciate it, Doc," I muttered. "But you should focus on the young men and women who are suffering. I've lived like this for as long as I can remember, so ..." I trailed off.

The doctor exhibited his best bedside manner. He put his hand on my shoulder and gently asked me, "But wouldn't you like to feel better?"

"Yes," was the only thing I could say.

And with that, it was decided. I would begin the treatment.

The Next Steps Toward Recovery

A few months after beginning the treatment, I underwent a second WAVi scan.

The improvement and healing my brain underwent between my first and second WAVi scans were of a magnitude the doctor had not seen before. While my results were exciting, it was important for me to know why I had such a positively dramatic reaction to the protocol.

"Why do you think I have such great results? Why do you think my brain healed so quickly?" I asked.

"The same reason you were able to save your own life while unknowingly suffering from TBI," he said.

He had surmised that my Ice Cold Leader Methodology that I practiced over the course of twenty years had so fully conditioned my brain, spirit, body, and mind toward positive behavior that when I was given the needed catalyst (the TBI protocol to heal my injured brain), my entire being responded with a thunderous, positive reaction.

Now the process I described, the Ice Cold Leader Methodology, comes as naturally as I hoped it would and no longer exhausts me.

All of my experiences have shown me that this system works—it literally saved my life. Much of what you're about to learn in the following pages seems like common sense because it is common sense. But it is not common practice.

When people first begin to practice this awareness around emotions, the effect on their decision-making process improves tenfold. When the decision-making process improves tenfold, people make better decisions, and life becomes less stressful.

When you do something repeatedly, like recognizing emotions, you create a habit, and your brain begins to hardwire itself according to that habit. Eventually, you begin to do these things subconsciously.

Subconscious behavior is the reward for working so hard to create good habits. These habits eventually become intuitive, part of your personality that you don't even think about anymore. This allows you to move on to other behavioral improvements.

The process and wellness aspects of the Ice Cold Leader Methodology saved my life during a time when my brain injury could have led me down a dark path ending in suicide. In other words, it sustained me during the bad times. Even after healing my brain, this method has propelled me during better times. My life is better because I now execute Ice Cold Leadership at a higher level.

Everybody has gone through or felt what I have felt in one form or another. The point I want to make clear is that this process will work for anyone, not just people with Traumatic Brain Injury.

PART 2

THE PROCESS

Prologue

I HOPE YOU ENJOYED PART 1 OF THIS BOOK. ITS MAIN PURPOSE was to give a full background of how I developed my leadership process and wellness techniques. It was quite literally a matter of life and death.

Why read on?

Sometimes my stories can feel a little unrelatable—interesting and entertaining, but unrelatable. You probably haven't seen combat. Relatively few people have.

You probably haven't suffered not one but two life-threatening injuries while operating as a Navy SEAL. Even fewer people have.

You likely haven't experienced Traumatic Brain Injury or suffered silently and unknowingly for over twenty years. Although, as we are learning, more people have than we think.

You likely have not been told that the injuries you suffered should have, in all likelihood, led you to take your own life.

As I've mentioned before, the challenges we face are not in competition with each other. They meet us where they are in life. So, if what I've gone through seems completely unrelatable to you, I ask that you reframe how you are looking at it.

Physical, mental, and emotional stress plagues us all at some point. Yours may not be as intense as mine, but it still exists for you. It still needs to be dealt with. If it's not dealt with, you will begin to suffer the consequences of your inaction.

And that is the point! We need to take action toward the things that will cause us stress and spiral out of control if not dealt with.

Part 2 of this book is my process that has been proven to help deal with anything that ails you—physically, mentally, or emotionally. Everyone has problems that need to be solved, and leaders solve those problems.

It doesn't matter if the problem is personal or professional, big or small, "significant" or "insignificant." The following chapters outline the problem-solving process that will work for anyone.

Introduction

ROGER WAS CLEARLY FRUSTRATED. "NO PROJECT EVER seems to get fully completed. All we do is move from one fire to the next. Everyone is so stressed out that they've become lethargic and unmotivated. I'm not even sure what they are working on sometimes. My boss, and everyone else for that matter, is constantly on my ass to fix what is important to them. It's all becoming untenable."

This is how Roger, the chief technology officer of a services company that runs entirely off the platform he is responsible for building and maintaining, summarized his current situation.

"So, what do you do about it?" I asked.

"What do you mean?" he replied.

"I mean, what do you do about everything you just described?" I asked again.

Roger paused and thought about my question for a moment. Then he provided me with the set of nondescript, non-specific answers I've become so accustomed to hearing as I begin working with new clients. "I just get it done. I crack the whip. We come together and work for however long it takes to finish the job."

"Can you be more specific?" I asked.

"I just told you what I do," he responded with a tinge of defensiveness.

"You told me you crack the whip. What does that mean?"

Roger paused again to think. He is very mild-mannered, but I could feel he was not comfortable answering these very basic questions. "You don't know what I mean by 'crack the whip?'"

It was important for me to tread lightly because my intention was not to put Roger on the defensive, but I needed to ask him more questions so he could see some things for himself.

"I think I do," I responded. "Let's change gears just a bit. How do you feel when those things are happening? How do you feel when you and your team don't complete projects or are constantly putting out fires? How do you feel when everyone is on your ass?"

"What do you mean?" he replied.

"I mean, how does that all make you feel? What emotions are you feeling when those things happen?" I asked in anticipation of a familiar response at the mention of the word "emotion."

"Errol, I'm not an emotional person. I just get it done. I told you that it is stressful and untenable." Roger replied as he unconsciously rubbed his face and tapped his pencil on the table. Even though we were on a remote video call, I could feel his energy. It was a little uncomfortable, but I needed Roger to go there with me.

I continued to gently ask Roger questions about how he felt and the things he did. He acknowledged that stress wasn't exactly an emotion, but it was the result of many negative emotions. We were beginning to get somewhere. Roger then acknowledged that, yes, he had emotions. He just didn't express them in an overly dramatic way.

Roger shared that he couldn't describe in detail the things he did in response to his emotions or current situation at work. "It's just intuition, Errol. I've been doing it for so long that I can't really describe it. I just act, and it gets done … but not done in nearly the fashion or with the results I would like," he explained. Roger's negative energy was coming down a bit.

As we slowly turned the conversation to him and away from his external environment, Roger began to truly consider my questions. We put what Roger did to the side and just focused on how he felt. "I guess I feel frustrated," he said.

"Why do you feel frustrated?" I asked.

"Well, I guess because I want to do a good job, and it just doesn't feel like I'm doing a good job."

"And how does that make you feel?"

This time, the answers came more quickly. "Like I shouldn't be in charge. Like I'm not worthy of my position. Like I'm not good enough to do this."

"And how does that make you feel?" I asked again.

Roger didn't have to search for this answer: "Scared."

And so began our working relationship, in which Roger would learn a new way to lead.

This is how most of my clients feel when they start working with me. They know they need to change the way they lead, but they don't know what to do. Worse yet, the stakes are so high that they feel afraid of making the wrong move. The leaders I work with experience an incredible amount of pressure to perform, and yet they don't feel in control of the teams that are supposed to help them get to the finish line. They feel frustrated because their instincts for how to handle the stressful situations they encounter are not serving them well. They feel afraid because they are stuck in their current leadership behavior and have no idea how to do things differently. They feel afraid because they realize they would rather continue behaving in a way that is familiar to them, despite its ineffectiveness, rather than try a new behavior. Ultimately, the frustration, uncertainty, and fear lead to feeling helpless.

Because I'm no stranger to leading under pressure, I'm uniquely qualified to guide leaders through this experience. I graduated from the United States Naval Academy in 1991. I was first assigned to the USS Monongahela as a surface warfare officer, where I served as assistant operations officer. In 1993, I began Basic Underwater Demolition/SEAL training. After graduating, I served as an assistant platoon commander at SEAL Team Four and platoon commander at SEAL Team One. As I explained in Part 1, when my career was cut short prematurely after sustaining injuries on deployment, I was medically discharged from the Navy in 1999. Needing to find a job and struggling to understand and deal with the impact of my injuries, I joined the private sector, where I excelled in sales and management. After 9/11, and after obtaining a medical clearance for the nerve damage to my left arm suffered during the fall from the ship, I began working for the FBI in

New York City in 2003, where I investigated terrorist groups from Afghanistan, Pakistan, India, and the Former Soviet Republics. In this role, I worked with law enforcement and intelligence agencies all over the world, investigating and combating terrorists. In 2012, I transferred to the Newark, New Jersey Field Office, where I investigated public corruption and violent street gangs.

During my time with the FBI in New York City, I was a member of the New York SWAT Team. Being on the SWAT Team in the FBI is a collateral duty. As such, SWAT Team members are required to effectively carry out their duties as criminal investigators first and foremost. Despite being a "part-time" duty, the New York FBI SWAT Team was as good a combat unit as I've ever been attached to. Because of my experience as a Navy SEAL and FBI SWAT operator, I was deployed to Afghanistan in 2010 while an FBI Special Agent and attached to the US Army's 75th Ranger Regiment, where I saw extensive combat operations. Because of my conduct during these extensive combat operations, I was awarded the FBI's second-highest award for valor, the Shield of Bravery. When I look back at my career in the FBI, I'm incredibly proud of the work I did and how I used my Ice Cold Leader Methodology to maintain relative calm and focus and achieved success, despite the brain injuries I unknowingly suffered from.

I've told you about my brain injuries, but I haven't yet gone into detail about other poor behavioral choices I've made. My graduation from the Naval Academy survived two academic review boards for poor academic performance and several conduct review boards for less-than-conformist behavior, any of which could have ended my tenure at the school. The situation was similar when it came to my career as a naval officer serving as both a surface warfare officer (ship driver) and special warfare officer (Navy SEAL). In both placements, I was on the brink of being asked to leave the Navy for conduct unbecoming an officer. Drinking, fighting, fraternization, insubordination—you name it, I did it.

I was not singled out in any of these instances. I earned the trouble that found me. I am and always have been somewhat ornery by nature. The irony is that I was saved each time because I was also considered by many to be an excellent officer and leader. The dichotomy was striking and summed up by one senior officer, who pulled me aside one day to tell me this: "I won't be surprised if one day you are found drunk and dead in a ditch or if you turn out to be one of the greatest officers this Navy has ever seen." For every time I heard that I was an excellent leader from either the enlisted men and women that I had the pleasure to lead or the officers I served under, there was always a flip side akin to, "Despite the stupid shit you do."

I had planned on spending my entire career in the SEAL Teams. It was not to be, though. Two months prior to my brain injuries, I had entered into a fly-by-the-seat-of-my-pants marriage to a young lady I met in South America. She was Colombian and had never been to the United States before we were married. After my injuries, both of my arms were in casts, and I suffered frequent post-concussion headaches, so I was home a lot. This gave us the opportunity to engage in a never-ending series of arguments. What a shock! I mean, after all, we had known each other for a full two months or so. (Yes, I'm being a little sarcastic.)

Reputation is everything in the SEAL community. While my behavior was inconsistent and somewhat self-sabotaging, I felt as though my reputation was in pretty good standing ... until then.

As immature and feuding couples do, we looked for areas of weaknesses in the other to exploit and hurt. She did not have to look far to find mine—my Navy SEAL reputation. All it took was for her to make some calls to my SEAL Team Command and level some false accusations against me to chip away at my reputation. On what seemed like a weekly basis, I would have to stand in front of my commanding officer and explain, "No, I did not lock her out of the house. No, I have not refused to support her financially. No, I am not shirking my duties as a husband and human being." Because the calls kept coming, it got harder and harder for my Command to believe me. Eventually, I had to bring in my lawyer to show that I had voluntarily ceded all of my paychecks (keeping about $300 a month for myself so I could eat) and voluntarily moved out of the house (while still paying the bills), resorting to sleeping on friends' couches and in my car.

After I brought in my lawyer, it was finally clear to my commanding officer that I was not doing the awful things I was being accused of by my wife. However, in typical SEAL Team fashion, his response was clear and unambiguous: "What the fuck, Lieutenant Doebler? Get your personal life in order."

The poor behavior exhibited by my ex-wife and me certainly did not lead to a healthy environment for recovery during and after my medical leave. In fact, it led me to abuse my pain-killing medication and subsequently struggle to get off them. This was my dirty little secret that did not help my cause one bit toward the end of my Navy SEAL career.

I spent extra time at the hospital after daily rehabilitation sessions for my arm doing administrative tasks for hospital staff instead of heading back to the SEAL Team Command because I was so humiliated at what was happening. Rightfully, this did not sit well with my SEAL Team Command.

Here began the self-inflicted dismantling of my reputation. I was the one who decided to stay away because I wasn't courageous enough to face the embarrassment of what was happening in my personal life and how it was spreading to my professional life. My injuries were severe enough to be given a medical discharge. I accepted the medical discharge without a fight, finalized the ugliest of divorces, and left the SEAL Teams with my tail between my legs, feeling disgraced.

In hindsight, I now understand that this tumultuous time was fueled by the impact of my brain injuries and that addiction to painkillers is an all too common result of traumatic brain injuries. Some studies show that between 10 and 20% of people with brain injuries develop a substance abuse problem. The shame I carried about this weighed heavily on me for years.

As it turned out, it took several years for the headaches to improve and for me to get strength back into my injured limbs.

Like most people who are humbled by circumstances, I began the long process of self-reflection that has led me here.

After I left the SEAL Teams, I started to reflect on my successes and failures. Why had I found success, and why did I allow failure, or at least needless setbacks, to plague me unnecessarily? While I lacked the context I now have (that I was suffering from Traumatic Brain Injuries), I started to become acutely aware of not only what I was doing but why I was doing it.

So much of what I had been operating on was emotion and intuition. Sometimes my emotions led me down the correct path, other times the wrong one. It was the same situation with my intuition. Sometimes it would bring great success, but I was not able to replicate it consistently.

Time, reflection, and maturity play an important part in eliminating self-inflicted wounds, and as the years went on, that's exactly what I began to do: eliminate self-inflicted wounds. I did this by developing what I now call the Ice Cold Leader Methodology. I didn't know it at the time, but I was developing a problem-solving process to put myself back on track, one that literally saved my life. Through my time in the private sector and then in the FBI, I began to operate with more consistency. My stumbles came further and further apart and with far less severity ... but they still came.

After 13 years of service, I left the FBI out of massive frustration with its leadership. Unlike the SEAL Teams, where the expectation of good leadership is the norm and bad leaders are the outliers, the FBI is the opposite. It was my experience that poor leadership was the norm, and good leaders were the outliers in the FBI. Even though some of the best leaders I've ever met worked in the FBI, this wasn't enough for me to stay. I decided it was time to put my money where my mouth was and either shut up and endure the leadership I disagreed with or leave. So, I left. After so many years of learning the hard way what it meant to be a leader, I could no longer stand watching and being subjected to the largely incompetent leadership in the FBI. I wanted to make a difference in the lives of leaders who wanted to change.

As I began the process of putting together my leadership consulting business, I finally had to sit down and evaluate my life and decide where things went right and where things went wrong. More importantly, I had to figure out why things went right and why things went wrong.

In short, I came to realize that my life was made up of a series of concepts that repeated themselves, regardless of the situation. And then I realized that the concepts I was recognizing formed a process for leadership and general positive behavior. Every potential landmine in life, and its solution, could be found in this process that I had developed for myself out of necessity.

My experiences, and deep reflection and analysis of them, have led me to develop a leadership process that will help define what we as leaders hold ourselves and our teams accountable for. It is not a series of "must-dos," but instead, it's a process that is flexible enough to fit anyone's personal circumstance, lifestyle, profession, or personality.

Because the leadership process is so flexible, we can say that there is an art required to ensure each element meets your needs and the needs of your team or your family. It is not a one-size-fits-all process. It requires thought, reflection, and artistry.

What's more, as I became interested in how the brain works and how to use it to produce real behavioral change, I came to realize the elements of my leadership process follow the necessary pattern to literally rewire your brain. I believe the scientific parallels lend credibility to the leadership process, beyond the fact that I developed the process from firsthand experience and not some theoretical model. I don't claim to be a scientific expert, but I do cite the scientific parallels for each element of the leadership process, so get ready for a little science.

Welcome to the Ice Cold Leader Methodology. I have a leadership process that mirrors the science of behavioral change and requires artistry to make it relevant. If you don't believe your circumstances are applicable to one of the elements of my leadership process, you can look to the science behind it for validation.

I truly believe if I had been exposed to my Ice Cold Leader Methodology as a young man, I would have avoided a lot of unnecessary hardship—hardships I caused for myself and those around me who loved and supported me. This process was built on the good, the bad, and the ugly experiences of my life, a life that's been painful and flawed at times but also obsessed with what it means to be a good leader. I hope that you find what you need within these pages.

The Leadership Process Overview ... and Cold Exposure

LEADERSHIP IS NOT EASILY DEFINED. ASK TEN PEOPLE FOR the definition of leadership, and you will likely get ten different answers. Likewise, ask ten people what leaders do, and you are likely to get ten different answers. And all of these answers, by the way, may be accurate to one degree or another.

Similarly, the language and concepts we use in leadership present the same ambiguity. But they shouldn't. The concepts of leadership are simple. A leader must have full situational awareness and understanding, which gives them the ability to make good decisions regarding that situation. Additionally, a leader must make it clear what they will hold their people accountable for. While these concepts may be simple, the fact is that good, effective leadership takes a little more work than this.

Great leaders don't ignore their emotions and experiences or those of their teams. Great leaders don't assume their people will know what they are being held accountable for.

Great leaders don't hope their people will know what they are supposed to do. Great leaders don't rely on assumption and hope.

Great leadership and continuity among teams require something that is rarely found: a common leadership language based in process.

The process I'm about to introduce creates a common leadership language that allows leaders to define what they will hold their people accountable for. The key elements of the process remain constant. The beauty of this leadership process is that it allows for artistry and flexibility to account for a leader's individual personality, current and emerging needs, and static and dynamic environments. It is a process each leader can make their own while ensuring their team is speaking a common leadership language. It is a process that allows leaders to toe the correct side of the line that separates chaos and order—two states of being that are often separated by the thinnest of margins in the leadership world.

This process consists of five elements, with each element effectively building off the one before it. The five elements are:

1. Practice Emotional Awareness and Recognition
2. Practice Cultural Awareness and Recognition
3. Create Guidelines for Behavior
4. Implement the Planning Process
5. Meet the Resistance[1]

---

1 Pressfield, Steven. *The War of Art: Break Through the Blocks and Win Your Inner Creative Battles.* 1st ed. North Egremont, MA: Black Irish Entertainment LLC, 2002.

These are not five random, separate, and distinct principles. They all build on each other to create a common leadership language. Like any effective process, we cannot skip steps. If there is a distinct leadership behavior or concept you want to work on, it will find a home inside this process. In any leadership challenge you face, the solution will be found inside one of the key elements of this tried-and-true, battle-tested, leadership process.

Process Is Not a Four-Letter Word

Some leaders feel that process is a dirty word. However, a process allows us to identify where things went right and where things went wrong. When we can clearly identify where our endeavors and initiatives went right or wrong, we can identify specifically what we should continue doing and what aspects need adjustments. If we act on instinct or gut alone, without imposing any kind of structure or strategy, we'll never be able to quickly and accurately identify where negative behaviors or actions are limiting our ability to accomplish objectives.

People shy away from the word "process" because it feels too confining. They don't like to feel as if their options for action are limited. Even though we can all agree that behavioral guidelines (one of the elements of the process I'm sharing with you) are necessary for effective leadership, how do we decide which behaviors are appropriate for each individual workplace? Isn't it possible that certain behaviors are necessary for some but not for others? Should some behaviors always be in place, or can they change? In the context of these questions, a process can feel as if it's stifling instead of helpful.

That's where the art of leadership comes in. Deciding what goes inside each of the elements of the leadership process will vary from person to person and group to group. There will be a certain fluidity and flexibility required to find your sweet spot, and then the sweet spot is likely to change.

You may believe that some behaviors, for example, should always be in place no matter what. Good! It's your canvas; paint how you see fit. It is not my intention to tell you which behaviors to implement. It is my intention to stress the importance of establishing behaviors and then offer suggestions, guidance, and anecdotes to help you in your decision process.

Steps 1 & 2: Practice Emotional and Cultural Awareness and Recognition

Our leadership process begins with awareness. If leadership is nothing at all, it is the ability to make good decisions based on full knowledge of the situation at hand. Leaders must be aware of what they are doing and how they are acting. And since emotions drive our actions, we must master Emotional Awareness and Recognition—the first element of the leadership process.

In the first element, we focus on awareness and recognition of our emotions. In the second element of the leadership process, we focus on awareness and recognition of our cultures— what we and those around us do—without judgment, for better or for worse.

A word of warning: The first two elements of the leadership process will be the hardest to master and the hardest to swallow, but they are the foundation of great leadership. Awareness of how we feel (which drives our actions) and awareness of what we do (which makes up our culture) will define how we behave as leaders. Without this awareness, we cannot make the necessary adjustments toward personal and professional improvements.

Step 3: Create Guidelines for Behavior

Now that we have done the work of becoming aware of our emotions, cultures, and actions, we can begin the process of defining what we will do or how we will behave by establishing the third element of the leadership process: Guidelines for Behavior.

This is where the rubber meets the road in the leadership process. This is where accountability and action live. Remember, you can't hold someone accountable if they don't know what they are supposed to be accountable for. Guidelines for Behavior is where we begin to define what we will hold people accountable for.

The measure for creating Guidelines for Behavior lies in this basic premise:

If you didn't change the way you made,
marketed, or sold your widget, but behaved
in these ways, would you get better?

If the answer is "yes," then you have established good Guidelines for Behavior.

Step 4: Implementing the Planning Process

The situational awareness outlined in Elements One and Two of the process, along with establishing behavioral guidelines in Element Three, are crucial building blocks for leadership. But ultimately, leaders act to get results. Leaders don't act randomly. They act in a disciplined and methodical fashion. They properly delegate after defining objectives. They are able to question actions while still fostering initiative and autonomy in their people.

Leaders do this by having a plan. The fourth element of the leadership process covers the elements of a tried-and-true, battle-tested planning process. Cover the elements of the planning process, and you will find mission success. And at the same time, you will create a team of thinkers who act with initiative, autonomy, and precision.

Step 5: Meeting the Resistance

My leadership process is simple and based on common sense. If you embrace and implement its elements, you will find leadership success. Yet the people you lead, and even you at times, will resist it. Why? "The Resistance" is that unexplainable force of nature that stops us from doing the things we know we should be doing.

The elements of the leadership process will help you identify where the Resistance is coming from and how you can overcome it, both in the people you lead and in yourself. In the end, the Resistance will mostly come down to using a very basic behavior that will allow you to face it in a constructive, methodical fashion, void of overly emotional behaviors or feelings.

Finding Calm Amidst the Chaos

Earlier, I mentioned calm and chaos toeing opposite sides of the same line. The ability to fall on the correct side of this line as a leader lies in our ability to know the leadership process and then use the art to ensure we have made the process something that fits our unique needs and personalities.

So much of leadership comes down to how you personally react under stress and pressure. Throughout this book, I'll be walking you through the five-step process above. But I'll also be challenging you through physical exercises so you can learn firsthand how you hold up under novel and uncomfortable situations. I'll be teaching you to use cold exposure and breathing techniques as tools to identify and practice the art of leadership. The method created by Wim Hof, the Dutch extreme athlete, uses cold exposure, breathing, and mindset to transform you physiologically, mentally, and emotionally. Lest you plan to write this off as some New Age hippie propaganda, all of the benefits of the Wim Hof Method are backed by extensive scientific evidence.

So, what does the Wim Hof Method have to do with leadership? For my part, I began learning the benefits of breathing and cold exposure from Wim Hof in 2017 and received my instructor certification in his method in 2018. In so many ways, breathing and cold exposure have changed my life and my health—those are a given. But in so many ways, I have also found that they have great leadership applications. The cold and discomfort make the voices inside our heads loud, which creates a chaotic environment, both literally and figuratively. How do we calm ourselves while in an ice bath? How do we calm those voices in our heads? How do we create order and calm amidst the chaos of the cold and our inner demons?

We will use breathing and cold exposure as intellectual and physical tools to help us become better leaders and better human beings. The leadership process will help us manage the chaos/order continuum we battle as leaders. Breathing and cold exposure will help us practice elements of the leadership process so we can begin to change our mindset and the way we see and react to chaos and turn it into order and calm.

The five elements of the process—Practicing Emotional Awareness and Recognition, Practicing Cultural Awareness and Recognition, Creating Guidelines for Behavior, Implementing the Planning Process, and Meeting the Resistance—will establish your leadership language. That language will create predictability around the environment. When people are part of a safe, predictable environment where required behaviors and expectations of them are clear and unambiguous, everyone thrives.

Element One— Emotional Awareness and Recognition

WELCOME TO THE MOST DIFFICULT ELEMENT OF THE leadership process. Emotional Awareness and Recognition will challenge you and, in many cases, frustrate you in every aspect of your life.

We give so little regard to our emotions. We've come to believe that we've got a handle on it or that we've got more important things to concern ourselves with than something as trivial and juvenile as our emotions. We may even consider paying attention to and acknowledging our emotions as a sign of weakness.

Here is the quick answer as to why Emotional Awareness and Recognition is essential to great leadership: Emotions drive our actions, and our actions drive our results. As leaders, we are judged by our actions: what we do, what we say, and the results we achieve.

If we want to be in control of the things we do and say that impact organizational success or failure, then we must be hyper-aware of the very thing that drives our actions—our emotions. Without this, mission accomplishment may as well be left to a flip of the coin.

Emotions Influence Both Our Outer and Inner Worlds

Research tells us that we have between 60,000–70,000 thoughts in one day, and 80–90% of those thoughts are the same as the day before.[2] Seventy percent of the time, those thoughts are associated with the hormones and emotions of stress (anger, jealousy, frustration, worthlessness, fear, anxiety, insecurity, guilt, envy, etc.).[3,4]

Every time you have a thought, your brain sends a chemical through the body to match how you feel with what you think.[5,6] This creates a cycle between the mind and body better known as the mind/body connection. When you begin to feel the way you think, you begin to think the way you feel, the body creates more of those chemicals, and the cycle

---

2   Dispenza, Dr. Joe. *You Are the Placebo: Making Your Mind Matter*. 2nd ed. Carlsbad, CA: Hay House, 2014.

3   Bethune, Sophie. "Stress a Major Health Problem in The U.S., Warns APA." American Psychological Association, October 1, 2007. https://www.apa.org/news/press/releases/2007/10/stress.

4   *Rewired: Introduction To Your Brain*. Gaia Network, 2019. https://www.gaia.com/series/rewired.

5   Dispenza, Dr. Joe. *Becoming Supernatural: How Common People Are Doing the Uncommon*. 2nd ed. Carlsbad, CA: Hay House, 2019.

6   *Rewired: Introduction To Your Brain*. Gaia Network, 2019. https://www.gaia.com/series/rewired.

continues.[7] Unfortunately, the cycle continues with the same thoughts over and over, most of which are associated with the emotions of stress.

In stress, you are in fight, flight, or hide mode. When we are in stress mode, activating our sympathetic nervous system, our body sends blood to our extremities because that is where we need the energy to fight, run, or hide. This is a good thing in the short term because it helps us stay alive. However, when stress is our sustained state of being, the heart starts to function incoherently. Then the heart begins to send inconsistent messages to the brain, and we move into a state of imbalance or unease.[8,9,10]

Experiences create emotions. As human beings, we do not distinguish between an actual experience that creates an emotion or an emotion that can be created by thought alone.[11,12,13] To our body and brain, it is the same thing. So again, if 80–90% of our thoughts are the same as the day before, our mind and

7   *Rewired: Introduction To Your Brain.* Gaia Network, 2019. https://www.gaia.com/series/rewired.

8   Dispenza, Dr. Joe. *You Are the Placebo: Making Your Mind Matter.* 2nd ed. Carlsbad, CA: Hay House, 2014.

9   *Rewired: Introduction To Your Brain.* Gaia Network, 2019. https://www.gaia.com/series/rewired.

10   Dispenza, Dr. Joe. *Becoming Supernatural: How Common People Are Doing the Uncommon.* 2nd ed. Carlsbad, CA: Hay House, 2019.

11   Dispenza, Dr. Joe. *You Are the Placebo: Making Your Mind Matter.* 2nd ed. Carlsbad, CA: Hay House, 2014.

12   *Rewired: What Is Change?* Gaia Network, 2019. https://www.gaia.com/series/rewired.

13   Hamilton, David R. "Real vs Imaginary in the Brain and Body." https://drdavidhamilton.com/real-vs-imaginary-in-the-brain-and-body/. Hamilton, David R. Using Science to Inspire, February 19, 2019. https://drdavidhamilton.com/.

body will believe they are in the same past experience all the time. It ultimately has nothing to do with the current event or experience. It's about the emotion that is created from the event or experience because the emotion will emanate and begin to define you from the past experience.

When you learn something new, the neurons in your brain make new synaptic connections.[14] It's a phenomenon in neuroscience called neuroplasticity, which tells us that physical and chemical changes take place in the brain from every new thought, choice, experience, and emotion.[15,16] To remember the new information, we must continue to revisit it ... like we revisit those emotions of stress day after day. When we do this, those synaptic connections in the brain become stronger and stronger, for better or for worse.

We very rarely get past our analytical brain on a day-to-day basis.[17] We are constantly thinking about what happened earlier in the day or yesterday and what we need to do next. When we are doing this during our workday, it creates a stress response that activates our sympathetic nervous system or our fight-or-flight responses. This is all OK; we need this to

---

14   Dispenza, Dr. Joe. *You Are the Placebo: Making Your Mind Matter.* 2nd ed. Carlsbad, CA: Hay House, 2014.

15   Doidge, Norman. *The Brain That Changes Itself: Stories of Personal Triumph from the Frontiers of Brain Science.* 1st ed. New York, NY: Penguin Group, 2007.

16   *Rewired: Introduction To Your Brain.* Gaia Network, 2019. https://www.gaia.com/series/rewired.

17   *Rewired: Demystifying Meditation.* Gaia Network, 2019. https://www.gaia.com/series/rewired.

survive.[18,19] But when this is all we do, all day, every day, the science of epigenetics tells us that this constant stress down-regulates our genes. When genes are downregulated, we get sick. In short, our thoughts (what happened yesterday or this morning, what we need to do later, etc.) can make us sick.[20]

About 5% of people are born with true genetic disorders. About 95% of people who walk into a healthcare facility do so because of a stress-related disorder.[21] Now that we know when we experience an emotion, the brain sends a chemical to the body, and that we think the same thoughts as the day before 90% of the time, we can rightly conclude that we become chemically addicted to our emotions.[22] And we know that the majority of us are acting on the emotions of stress about 70% of the time.

In essence, we use the problems and conditions in our lives to reaffirm our addiction to our emotions. We find something in every interaction or experience that allows us to feel the way

---

18   Dispenza, Dr. Joe. *Breaking the Habit of Being Yourself: How to Lose Your Mind and Create a New One.* 1st ed. Carlsbad, CA: Hay House, 2012.

19   *Rewired: Survival vs Creation.* Gaia Network, 2019. https://www.gaia.com/series/rewired.

20   Dispenza, Dr. Joe. *Becoming Supernatural: How Common People Are Doing the Uncommon.* 2nd ed. Carlsbad, CA: Hay House, 2019.

21   Dispenza, Dr. Joe. *Breaking the Habit of Being Yourself: How to Lose Your Mind and Create a New One.* 1st ed. Carlsbad, CA: Hay House, 2012.

22   Dispenza, Dr. Joe. *You Are the Placebo: Making Your Mind Matter.* 2nd ed. Carlsbad, CA: Hay House, 2014.

we've conditioned our mind and body to feel. We literally turn on the stress response by thought alone.[23,24]

Because the stress response downregulates genes, and this makes us sick, we rightly conclude that our thoughts and emotions can make us sick—or the wrong, sustained emotions, like those of stress. The evidence suggests the opposite is true, as well. Elevated emotions like love, gratitude, abundance, and worthiness can upregulate our genes and make us well.[25]

The Importance of Self-Reflection

Every good leadership process starts with self-reflection. Recognizing your emotions will allow you to act in a way that is in your control, not in a way that is in the emotion's control.

Our goal here is not to understand why you have the emotions you have. I do believe it's worth it for everyone at some point to understand the cause of their underlying emotions, especially the negative ones that drive us to act outside of our best interest or outside of our best selves. For some, this can be an exhaustive process that may take years. But again, this is not our goal right now. Recognizing your emotions and understanding where they come from are two different

23   *Rewired: Survival vs Creation*. Gaia Network, 2019. https://www.gaia.com/series/rewired.

24   Dispenza, Dr. Joe. *You Are the Placebo: Making Your Mind Matter*. 2nd ed. Carlsbad, CA: Hay House, 2014.

25   Dispenza, Dr. Joe. *Becoming Supernatural: How Common People Are Doing the Uncommon*. 2nd ed. Carlsbad, CA: Hay House, 2019.

conversations. We are focusing on recognizing our emotions so we can control our actions and make good, sound leadership decisions when that emotion shows itself.

As a leader, you must focus on the effect your emotions have on your actions. When we recognize our emotions, we can begin the process of understanding and controlling what our actions will be going forward. We are leaders, so we must focus on the effect our emotions have on our actions. Regardless of whether we understand the deep-seated root and cause of our emotions, we will still have them, so we have to be aware of them to ensure they do not control our decision-making process.

We are also not here to judge our emotions. You are allowed to have the emotions you have, whether you like what they are or not. Be at home with that notion! Again, where your emotions come from, how you feel about them, and how you act on them are all separate conversations. However, unlike the challenge of finding the deep-seated root of your emotions, recognizing your emotions and the actions they drive may begin to have a therapeutic effect on how you feel about your least desirable emotions. Minimally, you will eventually be able to dance with your unwelcome emotions when you realize you can control how you respond to them simply by being aware of them.

In short, the leader is aware of his or her emotions and then acts on them appropriately and consciously.

Where Do We Start?

Let's start by breaking down the word itself to give full clarity as to what we're discussing. The breakdown of the word "emotion" tells us all we need to know. The root of the word is from the Latin verb "to move." The prefix "e" connotes "to move away." Very simply, this breakdown suggests that a tendency to act is implicit in every emotion. Let's look at a few actions and some potential corresponding emotions.

How about when we procrastinate or exercise inaction? This type of behavior can be fueled by many emotions. Perhaps we have an underlying fear of the task at hand. Perhaps we feel overwhelmed by what lies before us. Maybe we are simply indifferent or bored at the prospect of what we need to do.

Fear, overwhelm, boredom, indifference—all are various forms of emotions that drive inaction or procrastination. If, in an honest moment, you asked yourself, "Why am I procrastinating?" your answer will lie somewhere inside an underlying emotion.

Let's look at cruelty or anger as an action. Why are people cruel? Often, people are cruel because they feel jealous of someone. People sometimes act angrily because they feel insecure or unsure of themselves, so they overcompensate with anger or even arrogance. Again, all the answers as to why we are acting in a certain way will lie somewhere inside an underlying emotion.

The theory of emotions driving our actions is simple. If we want to be in control of our actions, we must first be aware of the emotions that drive them. Now comes the hard part: How do we develop the ability, or habit, of Emotional Awareness and Recognition?

If leadership is nothing else, it is situational awareness, the ability to make good decisions based on a full knowledge of the situation at hand. For all the reasons we just outlined regarding emotions, situational awareness must begin with ourselves. We cannot be situationally aware if we are not in the moment, fully present, and aware of what we are feeling and doing during every interaction we have and every task we undertake.

For now, we are going to put the importance of being in the moment aside (we'll discuss it in a later chapter). Just keep the concept in the back of your mind until then. To be aware of what we are feeling and what our emotions are, we must always be in the here and now.

Like It or Not, the Emotion Will Not Be Ignored

Unacknowledged emotions live in our unconscious mind, which is different from our subconscious mind.[26] When we consciously walk away from a problem we are struggling to solve, we let our subconscious mind get to work. It's those times when—*BAM*—the solution just comes to you. That's your subconscious mind working for you.

Unfortunately, those unacknowledged emotions housed in our unconscious mind aren't getting the same treatment. It is easy to acknowledge and embrace good, positive emotions.

---

26   Sarno, John E. *Healing Back Pain: The Mind-Body Connection.* 1st ed. New York, NY: Grand Central Publishing, 1991.

We see children or puppies playing, and we smile at the joy and innocence. There is no reason to deny or put aside that joyful emotion.

But, what about the more troubling or negative emotions that enter our world? What do we do with those? Envy, anger, jealousy, anxiety, fear, worthlessness, guilt. What happens when we allow ego to take over and we deny we are feeling what we are feeling, as we typically do with those types of negative emotions? What happens when we ignore those emotions and bury them because that is the "strong" thing to do? What about when we push them to the side because it is beneath us to acknowledge those pesky emotions? Only weaklings acknowledge emotions, right?

Our body and our mind are the most amazing machines ever made. Everything that is a part of us has a purpose. When we feel an emotion, it serves a purpose. If we choose not to acknowledge something we've created, like an emotion, we don't get to just pull it out of our ear and put it on a shelf.

The body is a closed system. That emotion you are denying is going to be housed somewhere, and that somewhere is in your unconscious mind. It is not going to lie dormant until you decide you want to deal with it. The emotion will manifest itself in some way. It will manifest in a physical or emotional manner that you'll act on. And, if we act on an emotion that is sitting in our unconscious mind, we act without a conscious understanding.

When this happens, we are employing hope as a strategy. All you can do is hope your action will be appropriate because you are unaware of the underlying emotion driving the action.

When you are unaware of the underlying emotion driving your action, you are powerless to make a conscious decision about how you want to act on your emotion.

This is the process most people use when it comes to acting on their emotions: TRIGGER to EMOTION to ACTION.[27] Something happens that triggers an emotion, and they then immediately act on that emotion.

Here is the process leaders use: TRIGGER to EMOTION to THINK and DECIDE to ACT.[28] Something happens that triggers an emotion, and leaders recognize the emotion driving them to act, think about how they want to act, make a decision, and then act. But you can't add THINK and DECIDE if you are not aware of the inherent driver of your action—your emotion.

The (Potentially) Deadly Consequences of Unacknowledged Emotions

When I went to free-fall jump school as a Navy SEAL we went through extensive instruction before we actually jumped out of an airplane. None of it was overly complicated, but it was all important for obvious reasons.

We learned our body positions so we could fall through the air in an appropriate and controlled manner. Among other

---

27   Goldsmith, Marshall, and Mark Reiter. *Triggers: Sparking Positive Change and Making It Last.* 1st ed. New York, NY: Crown Business, 2015.

28   Ibid.

things, we learned the protocols before we pulled our parachute, which were pretty simple: Check your altimeter, look left, look right, look up, and look down to ensure you have clear air space, and pull your ripcord. Again, not exactly rocket science.

I walked to the airplane for my first jump full of bravado and borderline arrogance. In my mind, I was super calm, super confident ... Superman! The next thing I remember was falling through the air aimlessly and watching the instructor reach for my ripcord to pull it for me. I ended up getting to my ripcord first, but I had essentially blown through all my protocols and eventually pulled my parachute at the minimum safe altitude (probably a little below). In short, it was a disastrous and unsafe first jump that put those around me at risk.

My instructor was very clear when we met on the ground: "If you have one more performance like that, I'll make sure you never jump out of an airplane again." This was a tough proposition given that the SEAL in Navy SEAL stands for Sea, Air, and Land Soldier. It would be difficult for me to fulfill the "Air" portion of my job description if I was not able to jump from an airplane. He concluded his remarks by telling me I had twenty minutes to re-pack my parachute and be on the plane for the next jump. Essentially, I had twenty minutes to save my career.

That next twenty minutes needed complete clarity and honesty if I was to fix the situation. It was honesty and clarity that made clear to me that the bravado and arrogance I was exhibiting prior to the jump were false. It was all a lie.

I was not super confident. I was not super calm. I certainly was not Superman. I was one thing and one thing only: afraid. My action based on my underlying, unacknowledged emotion of fear was inaction. Inaction is not exactly a great draw for an "action" when you are jumping out of an airplane.

That's my point. Unacknowledged emotions create actions that we are not aware of until after the fact, if at all. Becoming aware after the fact, like what happens to many of us, can be too late to avoid a damaging result, like when you are jumping out of an airplane. My process in this example was TRIGGER (jumping out of an airplane) to EMOTION (fear) to ACTION (inaction).

But a funny thing happened when I acknowledged my fear. It brought the emotion from my unconscious mind, the place where unacknowledged emotions go to wreak havoc on us, to my conscious mind. Now, it was in a place where I could include "THINK and DECIDE" in my process and therefore make a conscious decision about what action I wanted to take. Simply acknowledging the emotion allowed me, not the emotion, to be in control of my action. And that is exactly what I did. I took control of the action.

I completed my next jump, the entirety of the course, and the rest of my jumps in the SEAL Teams in an excellent fashion. It does not matter that I never lost the fear of jumping. In fact, I made sure to acknowledge and embrace the fear before every jump because doing so ensured I was focused on the details to keep myself and, more importantly, those around me, safe.

I did not concern myself with the fact that after so many jumps, I still rehearsed all my protocols right up until the moment we jumped from the aircraft. In any endeavor, familiarity can breed a certain laissez-faire attitude. Among other seasoned operators, continuing to physically rehearse all my protocols on the plane before the jump tended to look a little out of place.

I could have been at risk of falling back into my original trap of overcompensating for my fear by acting with that same bravado and arrogance from my very first jump. I knew, however, that I could not trust that instinct. I had to focus on being aware of the emotion, thinking and deciding how I wanted to act, and then focusing on the actions I decided on. In other words, I decide on my actions, not the emotion.

Combat provides a heightened awareness of the consequences of our actions but also shows that the decision-making process for every decision we make is the same or, at least, should be the same—TRIGGER to EMOTION to THINK and DECIDE to ACT.

Many different things can happen inside of THINK and DECIDE. We can think about the Behavioral Guidelines we've established for ourselves or the Planning Process, elements of the leadership process we will cover in detail later. The bottom line, though, is that I was able to focus on the protocols I was taught despite the fear I felt. The simple reason is that I moved the emotion from my unconscious mind to my conscious mind where I could evaluate the situation and make a conscious decision about how to proceed.

It's About the Conscious Decision, Not the Right Decision

As you can see, not acknowledging your emotions can be a recipe for disaster, whether it be a matter of life or death, like it could have been in my combat jumping example, or a series of small, seemingly insignificant poor or unconscious actions that build up over time.

This does not guarantee we'll always make the right choice. The aim is to make sure you are making a conscious choice. If you make a bad decision, at least you now have a decision-making process to look back on and examine where you went wrong. This process will allow you to make positive adjustments for the next time.

Even when we make the wrong choice based on a conscious decision, we win. You win because you made a decision to go with your instinct, and then you were able to evaluate whether your instinct was good or bad.

As leaders, we can't hope or assume we will make the right choice on how to act. As leaders, we put ourselves in a position to take conscious action by always being aware of the driving force behind our actions: our emotions.

One Side of the Emotional Coin … Actions into Negative Consequences

Our Reactions to Our Emotions Are Just as Important

We all have our own unique demons when it comes to emotions. Sometimes those demons come from how we feel about our emotions. Yes, we have emotions about our emotions, and very often, those are the ones eating away at us in our unconscious mind.

For instance, perhaps you have a particularly challenging relationship with a family member, like a parent. Perhaps they make you angry. You might even have acknowledged, publicly or privately, that they make you angry. Yet, you can't seem to break the chains of your anger, or at least how you act on your anger.

You go through the process: TRIGGER (my mother makes me so mad when she talks to me like that!) to EMOTION (anger) to THINK and DECIDE (I want to act courteously and with a smile on my face toward her) to ACT (I act accordingly, and my Sunday dinner is without incident, but I am not feeling any better about the situation, and the tension in the air is palpable).

You go through the process, and the tension seems to build with every day and every interaction. You find yourself short and tense with your own family, friends, or co-workers. You seem to find the same anger or frustration you have with your mother everywhere. The process isn't working!

You're right, the process may not work in this case because anger isn't the emotion seated in your unconscious mind. You are not leaving anger unacknowledged in this scenario, so your anger probably isn't the problem. Who doesn't get angry or short with their parents from time to time, for goodness' sake? What's more likely is the emotion you feel *about* your anger is wreaking havoc on you.

We generally expect to honor and respect our parents as we move through life. We also generally expect that we can put hard feelings of the past behind us, especially if we faced some unavoidable adversity growing up. So, when we have these expectations of ourselves as mature and forgiving adults, and we still feel angry toward Mom, we may really be feeling guilty about the anger we harbor. We may be resentful of how we are continually treated and then, in turn, feel guilty about being resentful.

The same scenario can play out in many ways when it comes to how you feel about how you feel. Maybe you didn't get that promotion or recognition for a job well done, and you feel frustrated about that. Or, perhaps you came up short on a big goal you set for yourself and you feel frustrated or deflated. It may not be the frustration in these cases you need to concern yourself with because you are likely very in tune with that emotion. However, it may be a sense of worthiness you are struggling with. Perhaps you don't feel worthy of success and you are further embarrassed, ashamed, and insecure about that very feeling of unworthiness.

My point is simple. Look beyond the initial emotion to get to your unconscious mind because those emotions—how we feel about how we feel—can cut deep and wreak havoc on us.

Your question is likely, "OK, what now? Yes, I feel guilty about being angry, so now what?" Patience. One step at a time. Remember, each element builds on the one before it. For now, be aware of and recognize the emotion. It's the first and most important step. It cannot be skipped.

A Cautionary Tale

Without directly "addressing" emotions, my tenure in the SEAL Teams was full of emotional awareness and recognition. Regular respect was paid to emotions for battlefield evaluations, how you handled a short timeline, or stressful personal interactions of any kind. In short, if you acted on an emotion of stress, you could count on quickly being called out to get your shit together, plain and simple. The expectation of calm, methodical, and unemotional thought and action was the expectation of every SEAL, not just the leadership.

I also worked as an FBI Special Agent primarily out of its "Flagship Office" in New York City. The FBI is the self-proclaimed "World's Premier Law Enforcement Organization." While some of the best leaders I've ever worked with, worked for, or observed were FBI Special Agents, my caveat for that is that they were the outliers. As I mentioned earlier, the expectation of great leadership was the norm in the SEAL Teams. In the FBI, the expectation was the opposite. Poor emotionally charged leadership was the expectation and norm in the FBI.

When I investigated violent street gangs, I began an investigation into a group that had run rampant over a community for at least a decade. Various low-level arrests had taken place over the years, but none of them put a dent into the capacity of the gang to own the streets. This is primarily because the leadership of the gang did a good job of buffering itself against the efforts of law enforcement, leaving the lower-level operators to suffer the consequences of law enforcement actions.

My partner and I had recruited a well-placed source who had close relationships with many of the gang's most established and tenured members. Because of the source's access, we were able to infiltrate the gang with more than one undercover FBI employee. We did this through the source's introduction of the Undercovers to some mid-level, well-established gang operatives. To my knowledge from reading about the various investigations into this gang over at least a ten-year period, including state, local, and federal investigations, there had never been one Undercover introduced into the gang. I cannot even recall reading about one well-placed source in the investigations. In a relatively short period of time, we were well entrenched into the gang with well-placed sources and Undercovers.

Our goal was to get access to the gang's leadership so we could effectively cut the head off the snake. Once we had successfully infiltrated the gang, one of the Undercovers recommended a different tact to get to the leadership of the gang. It was a tact he had successfully used before and seen work on another occasion.

Instead of going the traditional route of starting with small, low-level drug buys in the hopes of moving up the ranks and eventually reaching the highest levels of the gang leadership, the Undercover recommended that we buy large quantities of drugs immediately. The Undercover believed that the strength of the introduction into the gang from the source, as well as several successful interactions with various members of the gang by the Undercovers, put us in a unique position to try this risky approach. We had successfully completed a couple of obligatory "test buys." This is where everyone is at their most cautious to ensure law enforcement is not playing a hand in the game. All was good. Now it was time to up the ante.

The Undercover's logic was sound: If we distinguished ourselves from low-level operatives, we would likely get the attention of the gang leadership quickly. They would hear about the large orders and begin to do their due diligence about the new players in town. They would most certainly inquire who introduced the Undercovers into the gang, how long the Undercovers had been around, where they were from, and the status of the buys already made. We were more than covered on all these fronts. One way or the other, we would know if we were going to get access to the leadership in a relatively short period of time. I agreed with the Undercover's idea wholeheartedly and prepared to present the plan to my boss.

This strategy was the epitome of risk/reward. From a purely administrative perspective, when you start with small, low-level drug buys and don't get anywhere, very little money is likely lost, and it is chalked up to the price of doing business. However, if you come out of the gate with large purchases that require large amounts of money, and you don't gain any traction ... well, understandably people in high places in the FBI will notice and ask questions.

What's more, while drugs were a sadly obvious way to begin buying from the gang, we wanted guns to be our focus. Gun violence was rampant, and we were now connected with the very players who were using and supplying the guns and, literally and figuratively, killing the community. We wanted to employ the same strategy with guns as we did with drugs: buy big early. This was all in a bid to force the gang leadership to pay attention with the hopes of meeting them directly and making a long-term dent in the gang's activity or stopping it outright. Risk/reward operations should come with lofty expectations, and we had them. Or, at least, some of us did.

Enter "Tim"

My plan was met with resolute dismissal by my immediate supervisor, whom I will call Tim. After I finished briefing Tim on our concept of operations, he went on to condescendingly describe the bottom-up strategy of gang work. We pursue low-level drug buys in the hopes of rising up the chain of command and maybe even getting up on a wire. I acknowledged Tim's strategy because there is a general playbook to these types of investigations that should always be looked at first.

However, I went on to explain to Tim how that strategy had been ineffective against this gang at curbing the violence and treachery it had inflicted on the community for many years. Furthermore, I informed Tim that these investigations had been conducted by local, state, and federal law enforcement agencies, including the FBI. Again, I added, these were investigations by all levels of law enforcement that ended with very little success. Even more, guns had not been addressed in prior investigations. It was time to change things up, I argued.

Tim's response? "It's reckless, and you're going to get the Undercovers killed."

I then went on to explain that the idea was generated by one of the Undercovers and that he felt completely safe given the validity of his introduction into the gang and the relationship he had built with the gang members up to that point. Further, the Undercover had previously, and successfully, conducted a separate operation with the same general concept of operations and felt we were in a better position to execute our plan than his previous operation. I even recommended Tim speak directly with the Undercover. Perhaps the Undercover could explain the plan better than I was explaining.

Tim ignored the logic in my argument and refused to speak directly to the Undercover. Still ever-so-condescendingly, Tim told me that the entire plan was a waste of time because it would never get approval above his level. Even in a parallel universe where my plan did get approved, Tim was absolutely certain headquarters would never approve that amount of money for ONE purchase of drugs and weapons. "Ludicrous!" Tim declared.

I might have further inflamed the situation by telling Tim that the plan called for several large purchases of drugs and weapons, not just one. Words cannot describe the look on Tim's face when I hit him with that one.

I further explained that I had already run the idea by the person at headquarters who would ultimately make the decision of money approval and who said I would very likely get the money approved based on what I had told him. Tim was not happy with my "insubordination" for running the idea by the "money approver" without his knowledge. I told Tim that it only made sense for me to talk with the approvers before we wasted time putting in the formal request. Based on my conversation, the money would likely get approved! So, Tim stuck to the notion that the operation itself would never get approved. My response was simple: "Let me request it, and let's find out. If it doesn't get approved, I'll let it go."

Given Tim's opposition to my plan, I asked that he let me brief the operation and field all questions. Tim agreed to let me brief. But he also went about the business before the brief of making his opposition to the operation known to his boss, who would ultimately have the final approval decision. Tim was also not shy about letting everyone in the office know how dangerous my plan was, how reckless I was, and how briefing the plan was a waste of time because it would never get approved.

Well, the operation was approved. Needless to say, Tim was not happy and began explaining to anyone who would listen, including the investigators who were assisting me in the operation, that I was going to get someone killed. This was not exactly confidence-inspiring behavior on the leader's part, to say the least.

What Has Happened So Far

Let's break here and reflect on some actions based on Tim's emotions. Tim showed himself almost immediately by flatly rejecting my proposal of big money buys early. Based on the things Tim said to me, it was clear he had never taken this investigative tact before, nor had he seen it done before. If he had, I'm quite certain he would have mentioned it. And if he had, he would have been able to explain the problems in my plan. Instead, he went immediately to name calling (reckless) and his anticipated outcome (I would get the Undercover killed). He then took the additional step of bad-mouthing me and my plan to those who were going to be directly involved in the operation. I know he did this because they told me (as if it weren't painfully obvious anyway …) and I walked in on him in the act on at least one occasion.

Tim's resistance to my plan wasn't the problem. The problem was how Tim showed his resistance.

Which emotions drove Tim's actions? I can only speculate, but I'm sure this behavior sounds familiar to some of you. Nobody who is secure in their position as a leader, or human being, goes right to insult and innuendo as their default mode of action. My speculation is that Tim's insecurity was at the root of his actions.

To be sure, there were risks involved in this operation. The Undercover would be meeting with murderers on a regular basis, carrying large sums of cash, and buying weapons and drugs. His only backup—me and the other members of the operation—would be blocks away and not likely in a position to save his life should one of the gang members quickly decide it was time for the Undercover to be robbed and killed.

If the risks cannot be mitigated, then opposition to the plan and overall operation is warranted. This was not the case. Suffice it to say, I was able to articulate how the risk would be mitigated. Whether you agree with my premise on risk mitigation or not, I always fully acknowledged that there was a chance the Undercover could be robbed, injured, or killed. Most importantly, the Undercover acknowledged there was a chance he could be robbed, injured, or killed. But we both understood and agreed that bearing risk was part of the job description and that we had accounted for every reasonable scenario that could put the Undercover at that risk. Tim struggled here. Tim was averse to any real risk, regardless of the planning and circumstances in place to mitigate it.

What is another term for risk aversion? Fear. If the emotion that drove Tim's actions was not insecurity, then it was fear—fear of being associated with an operation that held true risk, perhaps.

Remember, the problem is not the inherent emotion(s) that Tim was feeling. The problem was that he was reacting to and acting directly on the emotion. Gossiping, bad-mouthing, and innuendo are not the actions of someone who is conscious of recognizing an emotion and thinking before they act on it. These are especially not the actions of a leader.

What's more, Tim took the additional steps of continuing to bad-mouth the operation and, more specifically, me. Tim also did this at perhaps the worst possible times: during actual gun and drug buys.

"He's going to get killed!"

The Undercover was wired for live transmission back to the office, which acted as a command post for the operation. The command post was manned by some FBI analysts and Tim.

In this instance, the Undercover had a large quantity of money on him and was scheduled to meet one of the most violent and longest-tenured members of the gang for our first large weapons purchase. The planning and preparation were thorough, and contingencies, especially those related to the Undercover's safety, were accounted for. However, everyone knew of the inherent risks the operation held. The gang member could pull a weapon on the Undercover and rob him (aka, "rip" him), or worse, attempt to injure or kill him.

All members of the team in the field supporting the operation were well aware of the risks but were conducting themselves like complete professionals. I oversaw the overall movement of team members and communications in the field, which was being transmitted in real time back to the command post.

Despite the professionalism being displayed by the team in the field, Tim was not able to control himself back at the command post. Tim was walking around the entire office, not just the part of the office designated as the command post, ranting, "He [the Undercover] is going to get ripped! He's going to get killed!"

Despite many meetings with dangerous gang members, all involving large sums of money, the Undercover was never "ripped," and his safety never came under question during a gun or drug purchase. However, Tim's behavior never really changed from that first buy. Tim continued to act in this manner during the entirety of the operation.

When mistakes were made (and there were mistakes by me, to be sure), Tim used these opportunities to either attempt to shut down the case or highlight my "disregard" for some form of safety or procedure. When mistakes are amplified to an unreasonable scope, morale and trust begin to break down, which was exactly what happened. In the end, despite a massive amount of weapons and drugs being purchased (all of which were audio- and video-recorded), a murder-for-hire offer being made, and a request of the gang's leader to finally meet with the Undercover in person, the case was shut down with only a single arrest to show for it, leaving those responsible for the devastation of a community in place.

Why did Tim act in such a way to ensure such discord was sown throughout the entire operation? Why did Tim put the operators assisting me in the position to take sides ... agreeing with either him or me?

I have speculated that Tim was acting on emotions alone, without thinking about the actions his emotions were driving. I have speculated that perhaps Tim was experiencing some insecurity or fear that led him to act in such a divisive and irresponsible manner. With each success the operation saw, Tim seemed to grow more and more frustrated and, in turn, would seem to find additional things to unprofessionally criticize.

The Final Analysis

Tim was not wrong to feel the way he did. None of us are wrong to feel how we feel. The purpose of Emotional Awareness and Recognition is just that—recognition. We should never feel like we are not allowed to feel a certain way.

The purpose of emotional recognition is not to judge how we feel but to ensure our emotion does not lead us to act in a way that is not in our control. Maybe I'm being too hard on Tim. Maybe he was completely conscious of his emotions and how he was acting on them. If that was the case, though, then we are experiencing some other serious leadership gaps on Tim's part.

In the end, Tim's actions reflected his emotions, which were driving his actions. His actions were not those of a leader; they were the actions of someone who simply feels and then acts with no regard for "THINK" and "DECIDE."

Because Tim did not have emotional recognition, his actions led to discord and divisiveness, not success. Tim did not hold himself accountable for his emotions or actions. He just acted ... and we failed.

Tim could have spoken to the Undercover to get a different perspective on the plan when it became clear he and I were not seeing eye-to-eye. Tim could have simply said he was not willing to be part of something that involved the type of risk the operation had. The list of things Tim could have done as a leader goes on and on. But as a leader, he chose to forgo "THINK and DECIDE" and used the "TRIGGER to EMOTION straight to ACTION" formula.

For my part, as the case went on and saw success after success, I could have done better to take my own advice. I knew Tim would continue to act overly emotional with each successive operation because that is what he did the entire time. Despite his opposition, I was getting my way. Operations were getting approved, money was getting approved, and we were collecting an incredible amount of evidence. However, I grew tired of arguing with him over every little detail. I grew tired of him bad-mouthing me constantly. I grew tired of the wedge he was driving between the operators just by virtue of his role as supervisor.

Instead of acknowledging my frustration and maintaining my professionalism, I began to taunt Tim during the latter part of the operation. Every time I proposed a new operation, he told me how terrible and dangerous it was, which seemed to be a weekly occurrence. I could have simply ignored the insults and continued briefing the plans and seeing success. Instead, I began to take the tact of asking Tim to disagree with everything I said and proposed operationally because he was always wrong, and I was looking at his opposition as my good luck charm. I unnecessarily poured fuel on the fire and turned a harmless campfire into an inferno.

As such, this incident goes down as one of the most destructive instances of a leader not having Emotional Awareness and Recognition I have ever experienced. What was more disturbing was the number of allies Tim was able to recruit in his childish escapade, which goes to the fact that, for better or worse, the leader will set the behavioral tone. This story marked the end of my FBI career. The organization looked too familiar to me from a negative leadership and cultural perspective.

CHAPTER 12

Practicing the Other Side of the Emotional Coin ... with an Ice Bath

NO BEHAVIOR OPERATES IN A BUBBLE. IN OTHER WORDS, there are always residual effects to any behavior you exhibit, both good and bad. In this case, when you become adept at being emotionally aware and using that awareness to make conscious decisions as opposed to letting your emotions dictate your actions, you will begin to see that awareness in others.

Back a million years ago when I was a Navy SEAL platoon commander, my platoon failed its final exercise to determine our fitness for deployment. We failed because during the operational briefing, I had left out the radio frequency we would be using to communicate with each other. The monitors let us complete the entire two-day operation, only to tell us upon returning from the field that we had already failed the exercise after the briefing.

I was distraught, as well I should have been. It was inexcusable, and I was humiliated. The commanding officer came to my room after we had been notified of my failure. I don't know what he planned to say to me, but I don't think it was what he ended up saying to me.

He took one look at me and very calmly asked, "What happened?"

My response was simple because there was really only one response to give in my mind. "I fucked up. It's my fault. That's it. I have no excuse."

If he came to reprimand me, which I think he intended to do, he changed gears after taking stock of my emotional state. He saw that the last thing I needed was to be yelled at. There was clearly nothing he could do to me that I wasn't doing to myself, except fire me. And I was sure he would fire me because I believed I deserved it. Instead, he said, "Go do it again."

"The brief?" I asked.

"No, the whole thing. You'll be given a new scenario in an hour. Good luck." He left.

Our platoon had not slept in two days, but our energy went through the roof, and we began the planning, briefing, and execution process all over again.

A few days after we returned to home base, the commanding officer called me into his office, along with his second-in-command, the executive officer. They shared with me how they couldn't recall ever having seen a briefing and operation go so well, from beginning to end. Well done!

Again, the commanding officer took stock of my emotions. It was clear to him that I was prepared to absorb the ass-chewing I deserved for my initial failure. He saw this opportunity and let me have it.

The commanding officer saved my career and changed my life—not because he gave me a second chance but because he made the right leadership decision based on understanding my emotional state. He was entirely focused on me, in the moment, and weighed my failure against my reaction to my failure. He made a decision based on all the information he had available to him, not just on the one piece of obvious information.

At the same time, he raised my ability to operate on a higher level and brought me to my knees in a heap of humility and self-reflection. That's impact. That's massive impact! That's the type of leadership that disrupts the status quo. He understood the importance of recognizing emotions in others.

Would he have been justified in firing me? Yes, without question. But that is not the point being made here. Because of his ability to be in the moment and recognize emotions in others, he could certainly explain—with greater depth than a linear "pass/fail" criteria—why he had come to the decision he came to, whether you agree with his ultimate decision or not.

He didn't move straight to consequences. He held me responsible by allowing me to account for my actions. He asked me a question: "What happened?" Based on my answer to his question, he decided on the immediate consequence: "Do it all again, now." For me, the consequence was a blessing, a second chance, and a life lesson that endures to this day.

Practicing the Art Through Cold Exposure

Taking the time to practice anything can be difficult, even for the things we really care about. If you are reading this book, you care about leadership and want to get better. But the topic begs a very simple question: "How do you practice leadership?"

If you want to get better at the piano, and maybe even try your hand at a recital one day, you spend time alone on the piano and practice. You make mistakes, work on them, make more mistakes, work some more, and ultimately get better. Through this work and practice, you become ready for your recital. You don't just jump into the recital and make your mistakes there—you practice first!

Sure, when it comes to leadership, we must try things in real time and make mistakes along the way. It comes with the territory. But surely, there must be a way to practice before we give something a try for real. Welcome to the use of cold exposure to practice your art of leadership!

As we begin to work with Emotional Awareness and Recognition, you can be sure of one thing: Before, during, and after you step into an ice bath, you will have an emotion. And you will probably have an emotion about that emotion.

When we get into the cold, we experience vasoconstriction: an environmental experience that will cause some discomfort in our extremities as our body does its work to push blood to our vital organs so we can stay alive. Our fingers and toes are not as important as our heart for life, so the body naturally restricts the blood flow to those areas when we enter the cold. Additionally, the cold hits our body as a sensation.

Vasoconstriction (a little pain in our extremities) and a cold sensation in our bodies happen when we step into the cold. However, the emotions you feel when you take an ice bath are not automatically attached to vasoconstriction and the sensation of cold. Vasoconstriction and the cold sensation are just things that happen. You are assigning the emotion to it, whatever the emotion is.

Right about now is when people begin to declare that they don't do well with the cold and hate it more than anyone else on Earth. This declaration is an ACTION to your EMOTION that is being TRIGGERED by the thought of an ice bath or cold shower. For now, we'll put the excuses we make to avoid the cold on hold until we hit the second element of the leadership process, Cultural Awareness and Recognition. Let's stay focused on the emotions.

Nobody enthusiastically just jumps into a cold shower. Trust me, I've taken ice baths consistently for years now, and there is always trepidation or reticence. The initial emotions you have will not be deep-seated; they'll be logical, but you may not like them. Fear or anxiety will likely be the initial emotion, but you may want to explain it away because we don't like to acknowledge fear or anxiety because they are a challenge to our ego. Because of this, the secondary emotion may be a sense of shame—shame that you are afraid or anxious, shame that you are afraid to admit it, and shame that you didn't face the fear or anxiety and get into the cold shower.

Fear or anxiety are obvious, but try to go one step further into how you feel about these emotions. These are likely the emotions that will cause you problems.

Afraid of what? Who knows and who cares? No matter what the inherent fear is, it can't be properly addressed until we move it from our unconscious mind to our conscious mind. The unaddressed emotion sitting in our unconscious mind wreaks havoc on our actions. We do and say things without thinking because the emotion is in control, not us.

When we acknowledge that we are afraid, for example, we get to continue the conversation.

"Afraid of what?" you decide to ask yourself.

"Afraid of how I will react to the cold," you may answer.

"Well, how do you want to react to the cold?" you respond.

"With calmness, like it doesn't bother me. I don't want to look silly." Now we are getting somewhere!

"Well, how do you do that?"

"Errol said I will have a natural physiological response when I get into the ice bath, like when you lose your breath during a panic attack. But it happens to everyone, so I don't have to worry about that," you explain.

"OK, what else?" you reply.

"Then he told me to find my breath. Exhale. Focus on the breath and the breath only. In through the nose, gently exhale. Once I get control of my breath, I should find some comfort in the ice," you explain to yourself.

The conversation can go on and on ... and it will, especially when it comes to stepping into an ice bath. The point is, though, that it is the awareness of the emotion that is allowing you to have this conversation with yourself. You may still choose to succumb to your fear, but at least it will be a conscious decision and not some ridiculous excuse like your reaction to the cold is worse than everyone else's.

You can live with a conscious decision, based on an honest recognition of an emotion, not to do something. At the very least, it gives you something to work on, a place to find growth.

How amazing is that?

Otherwise, you are simply the person who makes excuses for yourself and pretends everyone can't see through them. In your heart and in your unconscious mind, though, you know the truth. This truth creates more unacknowledged emotions that lead to other behaviors you are not proud of or in control of. It is where we begin the all-too-common practice of beating ourselves up.

Find growth or more self-loathing? I'll choose growth by simply acknowledging my emotions.

Recognizing emotions and their potential effect on your behavior is a vital component of great leadership. Recognizing your emotions before you step into an ice bath is an amazing intellectual drill that will help make identifying your emotions a habit.

I have stepped into countless ice baths, cold showers, and natural bodies of water in the dead of winter. Each time I do, I experience an emotion. The emotion before I do is typically, "Ugh! Again?" Even after all this time, that is generally my initial emotion before I get in.

Sometimes it's excitement, like, "Yeah! Get some!" Maybe I'm in a calm, focused state. But, generally, I just think, "Ugh!"

That initial emotion almost doesn't matter to me anymore. Over the years, I've begun to assign different emotions to the cold, and I try to enter the cold independent of my initial reaction. I've assigned the sensation of cold as a catalyst to enter a deep, focused, meditative state. I recognize vasoconstriction as a temporary state of discomfort and a sign that my veins and arteries are becoming stronger, which will allow my blood to flow more freely and easily throughout my body.

When I'm super stressed, I imagine the sensation of cold literally zapping my stress away. When I'm super relaxed, I imagine the sensation of cold taking my ability to focus in a chaotic state to a higher level. When I'm distracted, I imagine the sensation of cold sharpening my ability to refocus at a moment's notice.

I could go on and on about the emotions I feel before I enter an ice bath and once I'm in the ice bath. In short, I go through a series of emotions every time I get into an ice bath. These are my emotions. They are not right, and they are not wrong. They are not necessarily what you should feel, but you can look to find these feelings if you like.

The point is, I can describe them vividly because I understand the need to recognize them so I act in a way that I'm happy with and conscious of. The reason I can do this is because I practice this drill regularly, every time I get into an ice bath. Now, it is a habit that I employ every day and in every aspect of my life.

Simply put, practice recognizing your emotions by stepping into an ice bath or cold shower regularly. How regularly? The physiological effects of an ice bath can last up to five days.[29] But we are not talking about the physiological effects. We are talking about the emotional and psychological effects. So, let's not kid ourselves. If you want to create a habit, start doing it every day.

Where to start? Don't worry, if you've never touched cold water before, you don't have to make your first experience a 32°F ice bath. You can start by turning your shower to cold for fifteen seconds right before you get out. You can start by putting your hand in a bowl of ice water for thirty seconds.

Remember, the drill here is to identify your emotions so you can act in a way you are comfortable with. If you are "gutting or gritting" your way through the cold, you are missing the point. Guts and grit are good but not how we want to go through our life. We want to find flow and calm.

Whether it's a cold shower, your hand in a bowl of ice water, or a full-fledged ice bath, there are some things that will naturally happen. You will experience that shocking loss of breath and extreme inhalation. Think of it as an induced panic attack. Rather, *recognize* it as an induced panic attack (an emotion). Without recognizing your "panic attack" as an emotion, you may be inclined to simply jump out of the water or let the "panic attack" control you.

---

29   Kox, Matthus, Monique Stoffels, Saane P Smeekens, Nens van Alfen, Marc Gomes, Thus M.H. Eusvogels, Maria T.E. Hopman, Johannes G. van der Hoeven, Mihai G. Netea, and Peter Pickkers. "The Influence of Concentration/Meditation on Autonomic Nervous System Activity and the Innate Immune Response: A Case Study." *Psychosomatic Medicine* 74, no. 5 (January 2012): 489–94. https://doi.org/10.1097/PSY.0b013e3182583c6d.

When we take the time to understand our emotions, we can make a conscious decision to exit the cold. But a funny thing happens when we come to our emotional recognition: We decide we don't like the idea of succumbing to our fear once we have faced it, and we stay in the cold.

We decide we are in control of our actions, not our emotions.

We find our breath. We slow down our breathing. We replace the panic-inducing, staccato breathing pattern with long, slow, nasal inhalations. We exaggerate initially, with long, slow exhalations through the mouth or nose. Then we fall into a normal nasal breathing pattern and enjoy our heightened meditative state.

Now, imagine taking that skill into your everyday life. Imagine the things you would not do or say because of some unchecked emotion or insecurity. Imagine your ability to act calmly and rationally in the face of external, chaotic circumstances. Imagine flow and calmness as your go-to state of mind. Imagine acting like a leader.

So, if you want to get better at identifying and controlling your emotions so you can be a great leader ... go take an ice bath, find your breath, and lead!

Element Two—Cultural Awareness and Recognition

THE SECOND ELEMENT OF THE LEADERSHIP PROCESS IS Cultural Awareness and Recognition. For clarity and to be sure we are all speaking the same leadership language, let's define culture. By definition, culture is the "set of shared attitudes, values, goals, and practices that characterizes an institution or organization."[30] Additionally, culture is "the characteristic features of everyday existence shared by a people in a place or time."[31]

In short, and for our purposes, culture is essentially made up of the things we do, not the labels we put on them. Before I explain what I mean by that, let me illustrate how the leadership process is developing up to this point.

Remember our friend Roger, from the Introduction to Part 2? Once Roger acknowledged his previously unacknowledged

---

30   "Culture." Merriam-Webster.com Dictionary, Merriam-Webster, https://www.merriam-webster.com/dictionary/culture. Accessed 29 May. 2023.

31   Ibid.

emotions, we were able to discuss his situation with some real objectivity and without the shame, fear, and insecurity he was feeling. His newfound self-awareness and vulnerability moved him toward curiosity. He understood that leaders must first be aware of what is happening within themselves before they can move outward and effectively influence what is happening in their environment and the culture they are building.

I proposed that awareness for leaders was vital and that awareness of one's emotions was where we must start for one very simple reason—because emotions drive our actions. Our emotions drive everything we do. If we are not aware of the very thing that drives our actions, then we are acting without conscious awareness and intention, and we are building an unintentional culture. If that's the case, then we are simply leaving the results of our actions up to chance, hope, or assumption. Chance, hope, or assumption has no place in the leadership equation.

Roger and I then focused on what he was doing, or how he was acting, based on his emotions. "I very often just do the work myself that is not finished, taking too long, or not up to my standards."

"What else?" I prodded.

"I end up giving a laundry list of things to do."

"What's the problem with that?" I asked.

"Now everyone just sits around and waits for me to tell them what to do. Nobody is thinking for themselves or acting with initiative."

About halfway through the week of applying cultural awareness, Roger called me and shared that he was having some difficulty identifying what his employees actually did, which is a completely normal revelation because we are typically not used to this kind of awareness.

He had a staff meeting scheduled for later in the day. I advised him to watch his team during the meeting and to pay attention to how things were being said more than what was being said. I advised him to pay attention to things like tone of voice and body language. For example, were people paying attention, staring into space, or doodling on their notepads?

During our one-on-one meeting a few days later, Roger was dismayed. He felt this way because he saw what his team did for the first time. "We talk past each other and make each other feel small," he told me. "I talk at them, not to them. I overwork the good employees and burn them out. I underwork the ones that need more guidance, and that creates resentment among the ones who are shouldering the load. My direction to my people is unclear and haphazard, if I give any direction at all."

At this point, I had to stop Roger. I explained that this drill was not so he could beat himself up but to gain an awareness between the connection of our emotions and the actions they drive. Roger acknowledged that he was not at all conscious of how he was acting, he just seemed to be reacting without intention or forethought. He began to realize that his fear, insecurity, anger, and frustration were driving him to act in ways he was not even aware of, which contributed to a negative culture he had no intention of building.

The moral of the story is that while he was initially dismayed at what he observed after having paid close attention, we could now go about making positive adjustments. But we could only go about making positive adjustments because Roger was now aware of what he and his team did, for better or worse and without judgment. By making informed and positive adjustments, he abated his overall frustrations.

Emotions Drive Culture

In Chapter 10, we learned about the vast number of thoughts we have in a single day and how many of those thoughts are repeated from the previous day. We also learned that most of these thoughts are somehow related to stress. The mind/body connection continues the cycle of manufactured stress, causing us to behave in the same ways.

To summarize this, if we have the same thoughts based on the same emotions every day, we will take the same actions. If we take the same actions every day, we will have the same experiences every day. We will experience the same workplace culture every day because of those emotionally-driven actions. The same experiences will create the same emotions and we will begin the same, predictable cycle over and over.

Because we are addicted to the emotions and actions of yesterday (and the day before, and the day before that), we will find any event, situation, action, or person to reaffirm our addictive thoughts and behaviors. When we do this enough, when we act a certain way enough based on our established neurochemical addiction, it becomes innate in us. It is now programmed in our subconscious mind and we do it without even thinking about it.

Welcome to what you do. Welcome to your personality. And it is a personality that you are barely aware of. We have become addicted to behaviors we no longer even think about or recognize. We think and behave in a certain way over and over without even realizing it anymore. Positive change can never come unless we at least can recognize the things we do.

Does this Scenario Look Familiar?

Let's say, based on what we've discussed, that you have become addicted to the emotion of anger or frustration. Something happened in your past that made you angry or frustrated, and you couldn't let it go. You thought about it over and over. Eventually, you may even forget the details of what happened, but you haven't forgotten the emotion of anger or frustration because you live with it every day.

Since you have now become chemically addicted to the emotion of anger or frustration and the subsequent actions they drive, but you have forgotten the actual source of your anger or frustration, you need to find a new source somewhere else. That's what addicts do; they find their fix to their addiction wherever they can.

You see your boss do something, and you think to yourself, "Look at what that jerk just did! He makes me so angry!" Addiction satisfied. Then you go to your co-worker and tell her what a jerk your boss is and how angry he makes you. But she doesn't feel the same way. She saw what he did, but it didn't make her angry. Then you think to yourself, "I can't believe she isn't mad at what that jerk of a boss did! Doesn't she care? Doesn't she see the injustice? God, she makes me so angry!" Addiction satisfied.

Then you find another co-worker and go through the entire scenario. Except this time, your co-worker agrees. Jackpot! Now every day, you and your new friend who share the same addiction can feed each other over and over. Anger and frustration now fill the air. Now it's what you do!

But you are not an angry person, right? It's just these people around you doing these stupid things that make you angry. Otherwise, you're an awesome, loving, and caring person who doesn't get angry.

Reality tells us a different story. To the objective observer, you have been angry or frustrated for as long as they can remember. At first, they thought it was just your mood. But then it persisted, and they concluded you had a generally angry disposition. Eventually, to the person who has witnessed you for an extended period and to the person who has just met you, this has become your personality. Acting angrily or in a frustrated way is just what you do.

What's more, think about the impact on your team or family when you consider the scenario above. Substitute any other emotion for anger or frustration in that scenario, and consider the consequences. Consider a combination of these negative emotions and actions of stress in your team or family: worthlessness, anxiety, jealousy, guilt, and shame. What happens if we, as leaders, fail to recognize the consequences of this pattern?

By the time we are thirty-five years old, 95% of who we are has become a set of memorized behaviors and emotions stored in our subconscious mind.[32,33] Isn't it worth it as leaders, and as human beings, to begin to take stock of what we do by exercising a little Cultural Awareness and Recognition?

Becoming Aware of Culture

In Element One, Emotional Awareness and Recognition, we showed that emotions drive our actions, and if we want to be in control of our actions, we must first be aware of our emotions. Emotions drive our actions, and now those very actions we take every day—the things we do—make up our culture.

What do I mean when I say culture is made up of the things we do and not the labels we put on them? Well, it's fine to say we want or have a culture of, say, "excellence." There is nothing wrong with putting that label out there.

The problem is too many leaders and organizations stop there, and that's unacceptable. If you can't define or articulate the things you do that create excellence, then you don't have a culture of excellence.

Before we do anything, we must identify the things we do that make up our culture—not what we should do, want to do, or plan to do, but what we actually do. As in Element One

---

32 Dispenza, Dr. Joe. *Breaking the Habit of Being Yourself: How to Lose Your Mind and Create a New One*. 1st ed. Carlsbad, CA: Hay House, 2012.

33 *Rewired: Demystifying Meditation*. Gaia Network, 2019. https://www.gaia.com/series/rewired.

where we focus on awareness and recognition of our emotions, in Element Two, we focus on awareness and recognition of what we and those around us do, i.e., our culture. And we do this without judgment, for better or for worse.

The reason we focus on awareness in these first two elements of the leadership process is that we can't make positive changes to anything unless we are aware of the things that need changing. The ability to make good decisions based on full knowledge of what is happening around us.

The Elements of a Good Culture

Let's dive a little deeper into what a good culture looks like. No behavior, good or bad, exists in a bubble. If you exhibit good behavior, it will inevitably create positive ripple effects. The same is true of poor behavior. Exhibit poor behavior, and it will create negative ripple effects.

Let's establish what a strong culture looks like. It will have two distinctive characteristics: it will be sustainable and transferable.

It's sustainable ... it's not lighting in a bottle. It's not the perfect storm of circumstances that come together for an instant that creates momentary nirvana. A strong culture sustains you during the bad times and propels you during the good times.

It's transferable ... it doesn't leave the team or organization when a core group of people moves on. People leave, but a strong culture transfers from year to year, decade to decade, generation to generation.

There are many examples of good, strong cultures out there in business, athletics, the arts—all walks of life. I believe I was part of one of those enviable cultures as a Navy SEAL. No culture is without its faults, but the overriding feeling when you walk into a strong culture, one that is sustainable and transferable like the SEAL Teams, is palpable. There is a clear sense of how things are done and that if you don't get on board fast, you'll likely be left behind.

The SEAL Teams: Sustainable and Transferable

June 6, 1944, or D-Day, was the Allied invasion of Normandy. It was a historical military action that turned the tide of the war in Europe, essentially ridding the world of Adolf Hitler and his quest for world domination. The problem was that the invasion of Normandy was the war's worst-kept secret. In preparation for the invasion, the Nazi Army constructed massive steel barriers, laden with explosives, off the shores of Normandy to prohibit the thousands of Allied ships and boats from coming ashore.

A gentleman named Draper Kaufman was tasked with forming a Naval Combat Demolition Unit (later to become the Underwater Demolition Teams, which still later became the SEAL Teams) to remove these massive barriers and effectively create alleyways for the ships and boats to land on the beaches of Normandy.

After intensive training, these volunteers were each provided a mask, swim fins, a knife, and a satchel of explosives. They were tasked to swim in before the waves of thousands of allied ships and boats, place explosives on the massive steel barriers, and create the needed alleyways for the landing. They would be doing this under the noses of the Nazi Army with essentially a one-way ticket. Their survival after they did their job, destroying the barriers to create the needed alleyways for the landing crafts to go ashore, was left to their own courage and ingenuity.

As such, they sustained a 53% casualty rate with nearly one in five killed.[34],[35] But they accomplished their mission, the invasion was a success, and the fate of the free world was determined that day. A culture was established that day with a seemingly impossible, some may say suicidal, mission.

Sustainable and transferable.

Let's fast forward to April 2009. Captain Phillips of the Maersk Alabama, a U.S. cargo ship, was taken hostage by Somali pirates off the coast of Somalia in the Indian Ocean. After a few days of stand-off between the pirates and the U.S. Navy, it became clear the pirates were going to kill Captain Phillips, and there was no clear way to make a rescue attempt.

A plan was concocted to fly in three Navy SEAL Snipers and their spotters sixteen hours and 8,000 miles from Virginia and have them parachute out of an airplane in the dead of

34   Couch, Dick, and William Doyle. *Navy SEALs: Their Untold Story*. 1st ed. New York, NY: Harper Collins, 2014.

35   "SEAL History: Origins of Naval Special Warfare-WWII." Navy SEAL Museum. Accessed May 19, 2020. https://www.navysealmuseum.org/about-navy-seals/seal-history-the-naval-special-warfare-storyseal-history-the-naval-special-warfare-story/seal-history-origins-of-naval-special-warfare-wwii.

night and into the ocean with their small boats and weapons. From there, they would drive their small boats to a large Navy warship, set up on the fantail of the Navy warship, and at the exact moment that the three pirates showed themselves in one of the five small windows of the covered lifeboat the pirates had escaped on with Captain Phillips, the three SEAL Snipers would simultaneously fire their weapons from one moving platform to another, killing the pirates and saving Captain Phillips' life.

That was the plan? Yup, that was the plan. And it is exactly what they did.

Sustainable and transferable. The time between the Normandy alleyway operation to the operation to save Captain Phillips spanned two generations. But that's what culture does. It transcends generations, missions, personalities, and capabilities. The only thing similar between these two Navy SEAL operational examples of culture is the seemingly impossible nature of the missions that were undertaken. The precision of their actions, however, remained constant.

The bottom line on the art of Cultural Awareness and Recognition is simple: figure out what you do, for better or for worse and without judgment. Do this, and it will be clear where you need to focus your energy for positive change moving forward. Fail to do it, and you will be left in a world of meaningless labels, bad morale, and poor performance.

Observing Culture, Practicing Awareness ... and Cold Exposure

My Early Exposure to the Culture

Young SEAL trainees are introduced to all sorts of physical, mental, and emotional challenges. I fared pretty well at those challenges at BUD/S training. I could run and swim fast, do a lot of pullups, pushups, and flutter kicks, and didn't particularly mind the cold water.

However, there was one area early on that had my number ... the obstacle course.

About halfway or so through the obstacle course, my forearms and my grip would get smoked. Then the second half of the obstacle course would become a series of T.V. blooperworthy falls from the obstacles because I simply couldn't hold on to anything.

As that painfully went on for several obstacle course runs, I began to adjust my strategy. I decided to pace myself. Slow down, I told myself, and that would delay the onset of the muscle fatigue in my forearms and grip. My strategy seemed to make things worse.

The first couple of times a trainee goes through the obstacle course at BUD/S, there is a little leeway given to them by the instructors. There is a certain amount of technique that needs to be learned, so the first time through the course is very much a familiarization run. The second time through the course, the trainee is certainly expected to have adjusted to the technique and successfully complete the course. By the third time, the expectation is that the trainee completes the course within an acceptable time. I wasn't there yet.

As I couldn't seem to get the hang of the obstacle course, things began to take a turn for the worse. I was beginning to attract the attention of the instructors. They were smelling blood in the water, and that's a problem for any SEAL trainee. As my confidence was being shaken every time I stepped onto the obstacle course, the instructors were close by to further demoralize me and attempt to send me on the path of quitting. Such is life at BUD/S training.

One day, one of the instructors approached me right before we were set to make another run on the obstacle course. As I was bracing myself for whatever mental, emotional, or physical pain he was about to rain down on me, he asked me a question: "What's the problem?" I provided the standard trainee-to-instructor responses: "No excuse," "I'll find out," "I suck." Then he shocked me.

He said, "No, really. Tell me what the problem is. Nobody can figure out why you are so bad at the obstacle course, and you need to get it right, fast." I explained the problem with my forearms and grip and told him how I was trying to pace myself to stave off the fatigue. I explained that I was practicing during off hours and just couldn't seem to get it right.

"No!" he shouted at me. "That's lactic acid building up in your muscles. You're giving it time to settle in and wreak havoc on your forearms and grip. It takes about four minutes or so for lactic acid to build up. Be faster than the four minutes. Beat the lactic acid. Attack it, Lieutenant Doebler. Sitting back gets you nowhere except dead."

I will never forget his response because, among other things, it introduced me fully to the concept of action as the default mode of operation. But it went deeper than that. It's easy to act when things are going well, when everything is lined up for you and confidence is high. It's another thing entirely to take that tact when you feel like you are giving your best, but things keep getting worse, as they seemed to be for me on the obstacle course.

I should have been able to complete and excel at the obstacle course challenge by then. I knew the techniques and was certainly fit enough. I was faced with equal sets of circumstances at play. My choices were to continue to pace myself and sit back, or "act." Like any good SEAL, I refocused myself, said "fuck it," and went for it. The days of obstacle course ineptitude were gone forever.

It's strange, the little things you remember that have an impact on your life. And make no mistake, the obstacle course at BUD/S training is a little thing. But I'll never forget it. I'll never forget the wink the instructor gave me as I easily finished the course that day. And most of all, I'll never forget telling myself, "That will never happen again. When I'm not sure, when I can go one way or the other, I will always act."

What Do Navy SEALs Do?

Now let's be careful because there can be a tendency to over-think culture in terms of what we do because we do a lot of things. Don't overthink it. Teams, organizations, families, and individuals have consistent behaviors that make up our culture. They do not include the occasional mistake, or occasional good deed, as the case may be. They are the consistent elements of "what we do," for better or for worse and without judgment.

From my perspective as a former Navy SEAL, what did the SEAL Teams do? What was their culture? Well, a couple of things on this.

First, we didn't have posters on the wall highlighting a label we put on what we did. There is nothing wrong with having posters on the wall doing this; we just didn't have them when I was there.

Here is an important point before I go any further: If another SEAL and I listed four things that SEALs do to make up their culture, we may each list four separate behaviors. But I'm confident we would look at each other's list and say, "Yes, that's accurate." Here is my list of the things we did that stood out to me during my time in the SEAL Teams.

First is that action was the default mode of operation. Given equal scenarios where a decision could be made to act or sit back, we acted.

Next is, "Yes first." If something was to be done, our answer was "yes." We focused on the ways things could be done, not on the reasons something couldn't be done. "Yes first," because there is always a way.

Additionally, we said "yes" because we had big, out-of-the-box ideas, but we executed them inside a disciplined planning process. The plan would tell us why "yes" and how we would overcome obstacles, not be bound by them.

Keep in mind, "yes first" was the spirit in which we operated. You obviously can't say yes to everything every time somebody asks you for something. Our spirit, however, was "yes first." We knew the plan would tell us if it was possible, and our ability to effectively prioritize tasks would make it an operational reality.

Finally, we worked unemotionally and methodically. I've never been part of a group that exhibited more passion and enthusiasm for work and life. However, when the time came to work, emotions were checked, and we methodically went about the business of mission accomplishment.

What cultural label do we put on that? Beats me! The important thing is that I can tell you what we did. That was our culture.

How It Translates

Let's take a closer look at how I described the Navy SEAL culture. Is there anything in there that wouldn't work for your organization, team, or family?

Your significant other asks if you can do them a favor, and before they even explain what the favor is, you say, "Yes, of course, I can do you a favor." Yes first.

You are having a big Thanksgiving dinner with your family. When the inevitable cleanup starts, instead of asking the obligatory, "Do you need help?" (which you probably don't mean because ... of course they need help!) you simply jump in and act. You wipe down the counter, take out the garbage, sweep the floor, whatever it takes. Your default mode of operation is action!

Do these two examples lend themselves to a good family culture? Yes, I think they do! Would they make a good business culture? Again, yes, I think they would!

Focus on Observation Instead of Conclusions

The purpose of this element of the process, Cultural Awareness and Recognition, is just that—awareness and recognition. Focus on conclusions later. For example, you may conclude that you have a culture of respect. That's fine, and it may be an accurate conclusion. But the art of Cultural Awareness and Recognition is being able to be specific about the things you do to create respect, which can be a little different for everyone.

What are the specific things you notice that your team does that lead you to conclude you have a culture of respect? Maybe everyone always says, "Please," and "Thank you." Perhaps you notice that nobody interrupts the person speaking. Maybe, when two people begin talking at the same time, they are both willing to defer to the other to speak first. If you were an outsider walking into an environment like this, you would rightly conclude that there is an obvious atmosphere of respect, and you would be able to specifically explain why.

Yes, positivity is better than negativity. Science tells us that negative emotions like stress, anger, anxiety, jealousy, and worthlessness literally down-regulate our genes and make us sick. Likewise, positive emotions like love, gratitude, abundance, and worthiness upregulate our genes and make us better.[36]

However, when we are looking for areas of improvement, we should focus on the things that we do that cause us to struggle or the things we do where we are successful in spite of them. It's fine to acknowledge the good things we do so we can keep doing them, but to get better, we need to be hyper-aware of the bad so we can make honest and meaningful adjustments.

This was the case with Roger before he made his informed and positive adjustments. When he said, "We talk past each other and make each other feel small," he was mostly drawing a conclusion.

I pressed him by asking him, "How?"

I knew he had done the work when he rattled off several examples of what he observed at the meeting. He noted that when people weren't speaking, they were sitting with their arms crossed and were pushed away from the table—a classic

---

36   Dispenza, Dr. Joe. *Becoming Supernatural: How Common People Are Doing the Uncommon*. 2nd ed. Carlsbad, CA: Hay House, 2019.

sign of disrespect to those speaking. He observed that any time a junior member of the team would generate an original idea or, heaven forbid, disagree with a more experienced member of the team, the more experienced team member would cite their experience to dismiss their more junior teammate's opinion. He concluded that if the more experienced team member didn't outright disagree using their experience alone as the reason, they would simply roll their eyes and slightly turn away from the junior member of the team who was speaking.

These were very specific behaviors that he had not noticed because he was either not looking for them in the past, or they had become so commonplace, he didn't even consider them at all. He summed up what he observed as talking past each other and making each other feel small.

Work Backward If You Like

We've all been to places where we walked into a room and felt a distinct energy, be it positive or negative. The same is true with people. We've met someone and truly felt an energy. We couldn't explain it, but we felt it. This electromagnetic energy put off by people is absolutely real.[37]

If you are having a hard time figuring out what people do in order to identify the current culture, work backward from the energy you feel, especially when it is a negative energy. Once

———

37 Dispenza, Dr. Joe. *Becoming Supernatural: How Common People Are Doing the Uncommon.* 2nd ed. Carlsbad, CA: Hay House, 2019.

you have this awareness of the energy you feel, seeing what people do to create the energy you feel will be easy.

The negative energy you feel can take many forms or carry many labels. The same drill holds here. Don't simply label. Identify the things that are being done to create the energy you feel. Then label it if you like.

When you feel a negative energy, and you see people interrupting and speaking over each other, moving frantically from task to task, and yelling directions or complaints to no one in particular, you can rightly label this a culture of chaos, for example. But you can only label it because you are aware and recognize what people are doing.

Practicing the Art Through Cold Exposure

Awareness and recognition are skills that need to be practiced in order to sharpen them. Just like each element of the leadership process builds on the one before it, so too does practicing the art of each element through cold exposure.

When we discussed Emotional Awareness and Recognition, we were clear on the fact that every time you step into an ice bath you are going to feel an emotion. To practice the awareness and recognition of our emotions, we must consistently expose ourselves to the cold and identify the underlying emotion we feel. When we do this, we come to realize that we can feel many different emotions at the same time, and they can change drastically from day to day. Once you've identified how you feel, next pay attention to what you do before, during, and after the ice bath or other cold exposure.

What are you doing before you jump into the cold shower? Are you pacing around the bathroom looking for something else to do like brush your teeth again or look for those darn nail clippers because you may want to trim your fingernails later this month? Are you spending an extraordinary amount of time on your phone browsing social media only to realize you are now running late ... so you'll do the cold part of the shower tomorrow? Did you skip the shower altogether? Did you decide to get the water just a little cold because you want to allow yourself the opportunity to ease into it?

In other words, did you procrastinate or make excuses to avoid the cold exposure? Did you procrastinate and make excuses not to do the hard thing?

When you jumped in the cold shower or ice bath, did you make a real show of it? Did you lace your time in the cold with expletives, "Oh fuck, oh shit, oh fuck, oh shit!" or some other overly-dramatic form of expression to signify how terrible it all is for you? Did you forgo any real effort to find your breath and relax and just go directly to bracing all your muscles, gritting your teeth, and clenching your jaw to survive?

When you exited the cold, did you run for a towel or a robe immediately and hunker down into survival mode until you started to warm up a little? Did you make a point to tell the first person who would listen how dramatic your cold exposure experience was?

It may sound like I'm being overly critical if you did some or all the things I'm describing. Rest assured, I'm not criticizing or judging in any way. I listed these possible actions because they are typical. The point here is to be aware of them. Why is it important to be aware of what we do before, during, and after cold exposure? Because it is likely a mirror of what you do during stress in your daily life.

So, if you are having trouble figuring out what you do during your day to identify your culture, this cold exposure drill will help you be more aware. Again, it is an intellectual drill to help you become more aware in a safe learning environment. Once we figure out what we actually do, we can then begin to decide what we want to do or how we want to behave (coming soon in the next element, Guidelines For Behavior!)

In short, if you want to practice the art of Cultural Awareness and Recognition, get into an ice bath or cold shower and identify what you do, for better or worse, without judgment!

This element of the leadership process allows us to see how things actually are. Without this realization, we cannot make targeted, necessary, and effective change. Without this realization, we cannot make the kind of change or adjustments that leaders make because leaders first see things for how they are, not how they want them to be (that comes next!).

Managing the Extremes and the In-betweens— Being in the Moment

B Y 2017, I HAD LEFT THE FBI AND STARTED MY LEADERSHIP consulting firm. I arrived at a client meeting in the city of brotherly love (Philadelphia) a little early, so I ducked into a coffee shop to kill some time and read a book by Simon Sinek called *Leaders Eat Last*.

The book began with a story of a pilot whose nickname was Johnny Bravo. In the story, Johnny Bravo was providing air support for a Special Operations Unit patrolling in Afghanistan. As the story moves along, Johnny Bravo describes how the unit he was supporting patrolled into a narrow canyon that left them dangerously exposed to all manner of enemy aggression. What's more, a fog had settled over the top of the canyon, which obstructed Johnny Bravo's view of the patrol and his ability to properly support them from his aircraft.

As Johnny Bravo deftly maneuvered his aircraft underneath the fog over the canyon to get a better view of the patrol, he realized he was witnessing the patrol in a gunfight. They had been ambushed. From there, I was enthralled with Johnny

Bravo's ability and bravery as he maneuvered underneath the clouds inside the narrow canyon to provide fire support for the Special Operators fighting for their lives on the ground.

I was immersed in the story. First of all, how can you not love a story about somebody nicknamed Johnny Bravo? But mostly, I was enjoying the story because it was familiar to me. I recognized all the elements of this story on a personal level. Patrolling with a Special Operations Unit into a dangerously exposed area. The vision of the high walls of a mountainous canyon that offer an enemy combatant the perfect vantage point to wreak havoc on a patrol. Ambushes, firefights, and the presence of a night fog in enemy territory.

I was engrossed! The writing was beautiful and the story inspiring—until I was snapped out of my trance by my hands shaking and sweat pouring off my face onto the pages of the book. I was in the throes of a panic attack in the middle of a city coffee shop packed with customers on their way to work.

We'll come back to this ...

The Science of Being in the Moment: You Don't Have to Be a Hippie

As we've discussed, awareness and recognition are skills. As such, they are skills that need to be practiced and honed. We've discussed practicing the art of awareness and recognition through cold exposure and the science behind the emotional and cultural aspects of awareness and recognition. What we need to touch on now is the skill that allows you to practice the skills of awareness and recognition—being in the moment.

In the West, the notion of being in the moment has long been associated with "woo-woo, hippie propaganda," monks, weirdos, and other human outliers who spend their time sitting around, not contributing to society, and too afraid or lazy to join the daily grind, better known as the rat race.

This notion is the very reason why I include so much science in this process of leadership. It allows the cynics to see the importance of being in the present moment without feeling like they are being manipulated into a cult. The believers of this notion don't really need the science because they have experienced the power that being in the moment brings, but they enjoy the science because it helps them understand why they feel the way they feel when they are in the moment.

Combining the belief in the importance of being in the moment and the science behind it allows both groups, the cynics and the believers, to meet gently in the middle and find a blissful coherence and an understanding of the other's point of view.

In cognitive neuroscience terms, being in the moment is referred to as metacognition. Metacognition is essentially an awareness, thinking about what you are thinking about, having a feeling about what you are feeling, and being aware of your awareness.[38] If the feeling you are feeling is born of some

---

38   Dispenza, Dr. Joe. *Breaking the Habit of Being Yourself: How to Lose Your Mind and Create a New One.* 1st ed. Carlsbad, CA: Hay House, 2012.

spontaneous, high-energy event, like hitting a patch of ice when you are driving, it will likely automatically trigger an action, mental or physical.

This is the case with intense emotions. We all generally recognize when we are extremely angry, frightened, sad, or happy. We may not, however, be aware of the actions these extreme emotions drive, like slamming on the brakes when we hit that patch of ice. The key, for our purposes, is to practice metacognition at all times, not just on the extremes, because life is generally happening between the extremes.

The Basic Effects of Being in the Moment or Practicing Metacognition

The more you observe, the more you can change. It's a simple truth. Have you ever seen yourself on a recording and thought, "My God, do I really act that way?" Perhaps you were recorded at a party after a few cocktails. You may think, "Next time, I'll stop after two!" Perhaps the wedding videographer caught you on the dance floor at your best friend's wedding. You may think, "I need to take that move out of my dance rotation." Maybe you saw how you reacted at your child's sporting event after your spouse recorded it and thought, "Maybe next time, I won't scream inane corrections to my daughter and embarrass her (and myself) in front of everyone."

You would absolutely change many of your behaviors if you could only see yourself in action. Well, we can see ourselves in action by practicing metacognition or being in the moment.

If You Are Not Present, Then You Are Somewhere Else

We've spent a lot of time discussing emotions. Emotions are simply a record of the past.[39],[40] We've discussed that we spend an inordinate amount of time on our negative emotions of the past, and, as such, we've become neurochemically addicted to them.

Because of this addiction, we are bringing the past into the present. Even right now, we are likely focused on an emotion triggered by some past event. And because of this, we now extrapolate that emotion into the future. We already know how we are going to feel in the future because we are bringing it forward from our past emotions. In other words, we're thinking something along the lines of, "Well, I'd better prepare myself to feel this way later today and tomorrow because that person or thing made me feel this way last week and yesterday."

Don't confuse recognizing the things you have to do tomorrow with how you are setting yourself up to feel tomorrow. These are two different conversations, and we now know that how you feel will dictate what you will "do." Will you be present, in the moment, and completing your tasks from a place of enthusiasm, confidence, generosity, love, and gratitude? Or will you complete the task from a place of past anger, jealousy,

---

39   Dispenza, Dr. Joe. *Breaking the Habit of Being Yourself: How to Lose Your Mind and Create a New One.* 1st ed. Carlsbad, CA: Hay House, 2012.

40   *Rewired: What Is Change?* Gaia Network, 2019. https://www.gaia.com/series/rewired.

resentment, frustration, and worthlessness? The distinction is clear, and it matters. Especially in leadership!

This concept seems simple when you read it. But let's not assume or hope we are aware of it all the time because science tells us we are not. In fact, science tells us we are the opposite of "in the moment" most of the time. If you are not in the present moment, you are somewhere else. That somewhere else is in the past you've become addicted to and the future you've become addicted to based on the past you can't let go of. This is a scary proposition.

Do One Thing Well or Two Things Poorly

As a former Navy SEAL, FBI Special Agent, and SWAT operator, I've fired countless rounds of ammunition from weapons. That type of repetition produces a certain amount of muscle memory to be sure, which is not necessarily a bad thing. But does an established muscle memory mean I can stop concentrating or being in the moment for each step of, say, reloading my weapon? Let's break it down.

Here are, in general, the steps one takes when reloading their handgun. If you are not a gun person, stay with me, and you'll eventually get where I'm going with this analogy:

1. Upon recognizing my weapon has run out of bullets, or "gone dry," I turn my weapon 90°, keeping it at face level.

2. I locate the magazine release button. (The "magazine" is the thing that holds the bullets and is held inside the handle of the weapon, aka "magazine well.")
3. I press the magazine release button.
4. I watch the magazine fall from the magazine well.
5. I grab my spare magazine from my hip, and I watch it as I place it into the magazine well while keeping my weapon at face level.
6. I press the slide release and watch the slide move forward, thereby chambering the round (bullet) and making it ready to fire.
7. I properly regrip my weapon.
8. As I point the weapon back at my target, I acquire my front sights.
9. I place the fat part of the tip of my finger on the trigger.
10. I begin to squeeze the slack out of the trigger.
11. I properly identify my target.
12. I pull the rest of the slack out of the trigger and fire.
13. I immediately reacquire my front sight and determine if I need to fire again.

This process takes probably two to three seconds for a seasoned shooter. Despite the speed with which this magazine change can be performed, the fact remains that these are all separate and distinct actions. Because these are separate and distinct actions, each action requires the shooter's full attention to do it correctly. In other words, the shooter must be fully in the moment for each action to ensure the action is completed successfully.

Even the best shooters get lazy and begin to rely solely on muscle memory alone for this process. It's understandable. In fact, the experienced shooter who relies on muscle memory may successfully complete this sequence of events to reload their weapon 999 times out of 1,000. These are pretty good odds!

But what happens when that one time you don't successfully reload is when you are in an actual gunfight and not on the range practicing? Does 999 out of 1,000 sound good now? Nope, not so much. You are now 0 for 1 and have increased your chances of getting killed exponentially. Your strategy at this point is to hope your opponent isn't good enough to take advantage of your mishap and shoot you dead.

As leaders, we don't like hope as a strategy. As leaders, we simply prefer to get it right.

The point is simple: why would you rely on muscle memory and risk getting it wrong one time when you can be assured you will get it right every time by being in the moment for each separate and distinct action?

One of the best firearms instructors I've ever had says, "There is no such thing as multitasking. You can either do one thing really well or two things poorly." If it is important enough to be in the moment on the battlefield when your life literally depends on it, then it is certainly worth considering during our day-to-day activities and interactions.

When we move from task to task to task, our brain moves into a state of incoherence that triggers our fight-or-flight response, or our sympathetic nervous system.[41,42] The sympathetic nervous system helps us in times of crisis to focus our energy. For example, if we were being chased by a grizzly bear, our sympathetic nervous system focuses our attention on survival: fight, flight, or hide. We don't need to be thinking of anything else in this instance other than survival. All our natural bodily functions move their energy to our limbs to enhance our ability to run or otherwise survive. In instances like this, this is a good thing!

However, when we "multitask" all day every day, we unnecessarily put our brains in a state of incoherence. We unnecessarily activate the fight-or-flight response of our automatic nervous system. We unnecessarily narrow our focus on only what is right in front of our noses. We unnecessarily move energy from our core bodily functions (like digestion, circulation, and reproductive systems) to our extremities. As we've learned, it becomes the behavior we are addicted to. When we are constantly in a state of fight-or-flight, like we are when we constantly move our focus and attention, our body moves to a state of "dis-ease."[43,44] Yes, we become sick, worn down, anxious, and otherwise moody and irritable. Not exactly great leadership traits.

41   Dispenza, Dr. Joe. *Becoming Supernatural: How Common People Are Doing the Uncommon*. 2nd ed. Carlsbad, CA: Hay House, 2019.

42   *Rewired: Introduction To Your Brain*. Gaia Network, 2019. https://www.gaia.com/series/rewired.

43   Dispenza, Dr. Joe. *You Are the Placebo: Making Your Mind Matter*. 2nd ed. Carlsbad, CA: Hay House, 2014.

44   Dispenza, Dr. Joe. *Becoming Supernatural: How Common People Are Doing the Uncommon*. 2nd ed. Carlsbad, CA: Hay House, 2019.

Conversely, when our brain is focused on one thing at a time, it relaxes and activates the rest and digestion, or parasympathetic nervous system. When our brain is relaxed, we view our surroundings from a wider lens. We can consider possibilities and create new opportunities. Internally, our autonomic systems (digestion, blood flow, reproductive systems, organ function) are operating normally[45,46] and not unnecessarily stressing the body or sending it into "dis-ease."[47,48] We are healthier, stronger, happier, and more clear-headed because we are not letting the emotions of stress dominate our being. Don't these traits feel more aligned with great leadership?

Consider the effects of the interactions you have as a leader when your brain is relaxed and open to every consideration. Consider the quality of your decisions when you can see the entire picture, not just what is in front of your nose for the short time you are considering options.

Now Extrapolate the Principle Out to Your Personal Life

My premise is that these principles needed for battlefield success are transferable to every part of your life, both personally

---

45   Dispenza, Dr. Joe. *Becoming Supernatural: How Common People Are Doing the Uncommon*. 2nd ed. Carlsbad, CA: Hay House, 2019.

46   *Rewired: Introduction To Your Brain*. Gaia Network, 2019. https://www.gaia.com/series/rewired.

47   Dispenza, Dr. Joe. *You Are the Placebo: Making Your Mind Matter*. 2nd ed. Carlsbad, CA: Hay House, 2014.

48   Dispenza, Dr. Joe. *Becoming Supernatural: How Common People Are Doing the Uncommon*. 2nd ed. Carlsbad, CA: Hay House, 2019.

and professionally. Have you ever had a disagreement with your significant other because you weren't paying attention? Do you have those confrontations when you are truly listening to what is being said and responding with thought and measure? No, not likely. Now think back to the times you have been in your boss's office or at a co-worker's desk. Remember when they were talking to you and at the same time immersing themselves in their e-mail or something else on their computer that had nothing to do with you? How did that make you feel? Less than significant, I imagine. And if it didn't make you feel less than significant, it's because you have been conditioned to accept this behavior as normal and acceptable.

Too often, those in leadership positions feel they have the right to multitask when someone is speaking to them. Maybe, as the boss, you believe you are hearing everything that is being said to you. Maybe you are giving good direction based on what you heard (or thought you heard), or maybe you are not. Because you have chosen to not be in the moment in the conversation, you can't say for sure if you've missed anything. Perhaps you are hearing the words, but are you missing the non-verbal cues that so often tell us more about what is happening than the words themselves? Now you will make a leadership decision based on incomplete information. You are not situationally aware, or in the moment, and therefore the odds of your decision being a good decision have been left to chance.

When we are in the moment with our conversations, we can recognize our own emotions and ensure our response is based on conscious thought, not on emotion. Having an emotional response is just like using muscle memory to change your weapon's magazine; you are relying on hope to ensure it works.

Remember, we are talking about getting the interaction right by being in the moment. If we get the interaction right, then we are in a position to make the best decision because it will be a conscious decision based on full knowledge of all the information at hand. We may get the decision wrong, but that's OK because we will have been fully aware of our thought process and can then make adjustments going forward.

Breathing and Cold Exposure to Practice the Art of Being in the Moment

When I conduct breathing and cold exposure seminars, I always ask the participants beforehand who has tried to meditate and who simply can't seem to get it right. Overwhelmingly, those who have tried to meditate acknowledge they can't seem to do it. The reason for this is that people have a misconception about what meditation is.

In the Tibetan language, meditation means to become familiar with your mind.[49,50] That's it! It's no different from emotional awareness and recognition or metacognition. To be familiar with your mind, you must be present and in the

---

49   *Rewired: Demystifying Meditation*. Gaia Network, 2019. https://www.gaia.com/series/rewired.

50   Dispenza, Dr. Joe. *Breaking the Habit of Being Yourself: How to Lose Your Mind and Create a New One*. 1st ed. Carlsbad, CA: Hay House, 2012.

moment to where your mind is right now. We can practice this through some basic breathing and meditative work.

Maybe someday, I'll write the Ice Cold Leader handbook for meditation, but not today. I simply want to provide you with a few basic guidelines using breathing/meditation and cold exposure to practice the art of being in the moment. This will allow you to master the elements of the leadership process.

Start your meditation for about five minutes (you can set an alarm if you need to). You want to focus on ONE THING. For our purposes, let's focus on your breath. It does not matter for now if you are sitting, standing, or lying down—just be comfortable. Inhale through your nose, not your mouth. I recommend exhaling through your nose as well, but if you prefer to start exhaling through your mouth, that is fine. Eventually, you'll want to do full nasal breathing.

As you begin your breathing, your focus is to remain only on your breath. When your mind wanders to something else, bring it back to your breath. It does not matter how many times your mind wanders. As long as you are familiar with your mind, you can bring your attention back to your breath every time. If your mind wanders fifty times in one minute of breathing and you bring it back to your breath every time ... congratulations! You are meditating. It's as simple as that.

What can you expect during the early stages of your breathing/meditation practice? Frustration, for starters. You will be shocked at how hard it is to sit for five minutes and focus your attention. You won't believe how many times your mind wanders. You will feel like you spent only .01% of the time focusing on your breath and the rest of the time bringing your mind back from where it wandered. Good! You're meditating. You are aware of where your mind is, and you are consciously bringing it back to where you want it.

Like anything else, it will take time to get good at. You must put in the work. When your body is screaming to get up and get on with your day, which it will, you must force yourself to sit still and focus on your breath. When your mind wanders, bring it back. Eventually, you will learn to focus on your breath to such a degree that you will finally get past your analytical mind and into your subconscious mind, which is where all of our creation and peace comes from when we consciously tap into it.

For now, though, start with focusing on your breath for five minutes a day, and when your mind wanders, bring it back. When you do this, you practice being in the moment. When you learn how to be in the moment, you will have emotional and cultural awareness. When you have emotional and cultural awareness, you can make a true and honest assessment of the areas needed for improvement. When you practice being in the moment, you will have full situational awareness and be able to make good leadership decisions based on all the information at hand.

The Cold, Too?

Yes, the cold, too. Cold exposure takes your ability to focus on your breath and learn to be in the moment to the next level because there is no hiding or lying in an ice bath or cold shower. The goal is not to endure the cold. The goal is to remain calm in the cold. Anyone can grit their way through it, but leaders remain calm amidst the chaos and use grit only when they need it, which is not as often as we think.

Remember, science tells us that the brain relaxes when it is present, in the moment, and focused on one thing at a time—not when it is scattered from thing to thing to thing. Think about where your mind scatters when you step into an ice bath or cold shower. "This sucks! How much longer? Why am I doing this? This is so cold! I want to get out!" When we think this way, we have no coherence in the brain because it is scattered. Thus, we will not focus our attention on one thing and remain calm.

But when we focus on one thing in the cold—our breath—we know that our brain relaxes. We know that when we consciously exhale, we activate the vagus nerve which serves to calm us down.[51,52] In the cold is where you test your ability to practice your breathing and meditation focus because if you don't, you will not do well. You will feel panicked, uncertain, and out of control. Again, not traits of a good leader.

However, if you move your practice of breathing and meditation to the cold, you will thrive in the chaos and prove to

------

51   Kox, Matthus, Monique Stoffels, Saane P Smeekens, Nens van Alfen, Marc Gomes, Thus M.H. Eusvogels, Maria T.E. Hopman, Johannes G. van der Hoeven, Mihai G. Netea, and Peter Pickkers. "The Influence of Concentration/Meditation on Autonomic Nervous System Activity and the Innate Immune Response: A Case Study." *Psychosomatic Medicine* 74, no. 5 (January 2012): 489–94. https://doi. org/10.1097/PSY.0b013e3182583c6d.

52   Falls, Jordan. "How to Stimulate Your Vagus Nerve for Better Mental Health." Optimal Living Dynamics, 2020. https://www.optimallivingdynamics.com/blog/how-to-stimulate-your-vagus-nerve-for-better-mental-health-brain-vns-ways-treatment-activate-natural-foods-depression-anxiety-stress-heart-rate-variability-yoga-massage-vagal-tone-dysfunction.

yourself you can do it under any circumstance. When your mind wanders in an ice bath, which it will, bring it back to your breath. Every time. Be conscious of where your mind is and bring it back when it wanders, and you will find calm and consciousness in the chaos of the cold.

Will it be easy? No! That is why we must put in the work. It is why when we put in the work, we develop a unique and enviable skill that separates leaders from everyone else.

Breathe, meditate, get cold, and learn to be in the moment!

How Did That Coffee Shop Story End?

As you recall, I left you with me reading and enjoying my book in the coffee shop only to suddenly realize my hands were shaking, and I was sweating profusely. The coffee shop was packed, and I was sure I was about to draw attention to myself if I hadn't already. So, what to do?

First, I recognized what was happening. I was in the moment and recognized that some extreme emotion had been triggered by reading the war chronicles of Johnny Bravo. I had Emotional Awareness and Recognition because I was in the moment and present to how I was feeling.

Next, I recognized what I was doing. Again—a form of Cultural Awareness and Recognition based on the concept of being in the moment, or metacognition, or meditation. I was having a panic attack! When I realized I was having a panic attack, I sort of double-dipped because I started to panic about having a panic attack. I was in a moment of chaos, to say the least. So, I followed a familiar process because I realized I had been here before. When? Every time I stepped into an ice bath.

The sympathetic, or fight-or-flight, response you get when you enter an ice bath is nothing more than a panic attack. Then I reminded myself what I customarily do when I get into an ice bath—I focus on my breath. I remembered that focusing on one thing calms the brain. I remembered that when I exhale, it activates the vagus nerve, which will serve to calm me down.[53] And I remembered that I have done this hundreds of times before in an ice bath, so this should not be any different.

That is exactly what I did. I focused on my breath and only my breath—not on the noise of my hands shaking, sweating profusely, or how silly I might have looked sitting at the coffee shop table. None of those things were going to help me. I breathed deeply in through my nose and exhaled gently through my mouth. By my second breath, I was calm. I had stopped shaking and sweating and was calm and in full control of my mind and body, just like when I get into an ice bath. Just like when I practice my breathing and meditation.

I went on to have a successful meeting, and when I arrived home, I shared what happened with my wife. She asked if I needed to go see someone. Was I suffering from PTSD? I was not and am not ever opposed to seeing a professional

---

53   Falls, Jordan. "How to Stimulate Your Vagus Nerve for Better Mental Health." Optimal Living Dynamics, 2020. https://www.optimallivingdynamics.com/blog/howto-stimulate-your-vagus-nerve-for-better-mental-health-brain-vns-ways-treatment-activate-natural-foods-depression-anxiety-stress-heart-rate-variability-yoga-massage-vagal-tone-dysfunction.

regarding this or any other struggle I may be having. However, I opined to my wife that the only thing a professional would do is try to help me get past the panic attack, and I already know how to do that. She agreed. Even worse, they may try to prescribe me some sort of medication to "help" my condition. We both knew this was not a road I should go down because masking the symptoms of the panic does nothing to fix the problem. And, again, I had already shown a full understanding of what happened and how to positively deal with it. We agreed to watch it for the time being.

I have not had a panic attack since.

Imagine all the people who suffer from some form of PTSD, anxiety, depression, or panic attacks to one degree or another. Think about the havoc it wreaks on their lives. Think about the power they are giving away to narcotics, prescribed or otherwise, that is taking away the power to heal themselves.

This is a true story. My hope in sharing it with you is to show how this leadership process allows you to thrive in chaotic environments and improve your life based on the simple concept of learning how to be in the moment, understanding how you are feeling, and what actions those feelings drive.

CHAPTER 16

Element Three—
Guidelines for Behavior

MOST PEOPLE CAN AGREE THAT BEING A NAVY SEAL AND
an FBI Special Agent are two exciting jobs. But one of
my favorite jobs was the one I held after I left the SEAL Teams
and before I entered the FBI: selling copiers. I took the job
because, like most people who take a job, I needed a paycheck.
As I explained in Part 1, I left the SEAL Teams after an injury
that cut my career short. I had every intention of staying in
the Navy as a SEAL, but it wasn't to be. I got into sales on the
recommendation of a friend. The same friend recommended
copier sales as a start because, as he put it, "It's the Vietnam of
sales. If you can sell a copier, you can sell anything. Plus, they'll
take anybody."

Not surprisingly, I was not excited about this job at first.
I played all the typical mind tricks to convince myself I was
adding value to society and that my job mattered now as it had
before. I was losing that battle. I never did, and never will, care
about copiers.

What I found that I loved, however, was the environment the
leader created. The environment was safe because it was predictable. Because the environment was safe and predictable, I

enjoyed going to work. Because I enjoyed going to work, I did good work. *We* did good work. Our team always outperformed other sales teams throughout the country, but not because we loved copiers. It was because we loved the environment. And because we loved the safe and predictable environment, and because the safe and predictable environment created social and professional successes, we all had a certain pride working for our copier company.

It was not a great environment because our team enjoyed happy hours and other fun events outside of work. We enjoyed happy hours and other fun events outside of work because we all treated each other with courtesy and respect in the workplace. We treated each other with courtesy and respect in the workplace because certain Guidelines for Behavior were put in place by our leader that he consistently reiterated and enforced.

We felt the kind of pride that so many leaders want from their people out of the gate. Leaders cannot will their people to have pride. They can, however, create the environment that will ultimately lead to the sense of pride leaders desperately want from their team.

By now you are seeing the progression of the elements of the leadership process and how they build upon each other. Good leadership always starts from the inside and works its way out. As such, we began with Emotional Awareness and Recognition because emotions drive our actions and we must be hyper-focused on our emotions in order to have control over our actions.

As culture is nothing more than the sum of the things we do (which are driven by our emotions) we must have a clear understanding of what our current culture is by practicing Cultural Awareness and Recognition. Only when we are aware of our current culture, for better or worse, and without judgment, can we begin the process of defining what we want our culture to be.

Guidelines for Behavior is where the proverbial rubber meets the road. Since actions make up our culture, Guidelines for Behavior now let us begin to define what actions to take so *we* can define our culture, as opposed to letting unchecked emotions define our actions and our culture. Every person, family, and team has a culture. The question is whether you've defined what it is. By definition, a guideline is:

1. A line by which one is guided, such as a cord or rope, to aid a passer over a difficult point or to permit retracing a course
2. An indication or outline of policy or conduct

As the definition shows, having an outline of conduct, or behaviors, serves to set us on our desired path and establish a place to return when we inevitably go off course, because we all venture off course occasionally. Guidelines for Behavior remind us where to go when we have to ask ourselves, "How did we get here? How did things get this crazy?" It will be a deviation from behavior that gets us off course, not some market-specific event.

Remember how we described a good culture? A good culture will propel you during the good times and sustain you during the bad times. Culture is made up of the things you do and how you behave. Therefore, Guidelines for Behavior is the first thing you should check if you or your team has ventured off course.

Behavioral guidelines establish the desired behaviors that make up our culture and set clear expectations. If we expect people to act in a certain way, we need to be clear about what that way is. Otherwise, we work on assumptions and hope. We assume somebody knows what to do or how to act; we hope somebody knows what to do or how to act without you, the leader, making it clear to them. Assumptions and hope have no place in the leadership equation. Clear and unambiguous Guidelines for Behavior do.

Who Establishes Guidelines for Behavior and Why?

Who should establish the guidelines? The leader establishes the guidelines because without clear guidelines, people will behave as they choose. It's your team. You are answerable, or accountable, for its performance. Therefore, you establish the parameters for its success.

This is not dictatorial by any stretch of the imagination. We are not asking people to not be themselves. Unless, of course, "yourself" is someone who exhibits rude, anti-social, or destructive behavior that will have an adverse effect on a team or environment. If this is the case, and we have established clear Guidelines for Behavior that people can't or won't abide by, then we can say with clarity and good for all sides, "You are not a cultural fit." Again, culture is nothing more than the things you do.

Leaders too often obsess over why people don't love or care about their job more. My guidance is always for them to stop worrying about what people think about the job and focus on creating an *environment* people can love. What environment will people grow to love or, at least, respect? One with behavioral predictability. If people are confident they will be treated in a way that is consistent and predictable, they will generally enjoy going to work because of the predictability the environment creates. Once people begin to enjoy the environment, they will begin to have more affinity for the organization and the work, not the other way around.

Just as a reminder that the leadership process is applicable in all aspects of your life. Take this premise home, literally. When we exhibit predictable behaviors as spouses, parents, siblings, and friends, our home becomes the place we want it to be: a place of safety and comfort—not because we say it will be that way, but because of the behaviors we exhibit. And to ensure which behaviors will create the predictability, safety, and comfort we desire at home, we need to define them so we can hold each other accountable for them.

Don't confuse environmental predictability with a job that is inherently unpredictable. Sometimes sales can be unpredictable. Finance can be unpredictable. Being a SEAL and FBI

Special Agent can be unpredictable. Being a parent or spouse can be unpredictable. What I'm talking about is the behavioral environment. If the leader expects one thing out of you today and a different thing tomorrow, that's an unpredictable environment people will grow tired of. If the leader treats you one way today and another way tomorrow, that's an unpredictable environment people will grow tired of. If teammates can vent, criticize, and demean at the whim of their emotions without having to answer to the leader for their behavior, that's an unpredictable environment people will grow tired of.

It's a hard truth that, for many, a job can be nothing more than a means to a financial end. People need to make money. Therefore, they need a job. The need to provide for themselves or their family greatly supersedes their need to love their work. There is nothing wrong with this motivation. By and large, the leader should not care about someone's motivation because they have no control over that. What a leader has total control over is the state of the work environment.

Establishing the Right Guidelines

So how do we establish the right Guidelines for Behavior that will define our culture, both as a team and as an individual? Remember, our drill at the end of Culture Awareness and Recognition was to be observant of the behaviors of yourself, your team, your family, and your surroundings. This drill enabled us to identify what our culture is, for better or worse. After we've gone about the business of identifying the reality of our culture, we then must begin to decide what we want it to be, if different than what it currently is. We begin that process by asking a simple question: *If we didn't change the way we made, marketed, or sold our widget, but behaved in **these** ways, would we get better?*

Your "widget" is your actual job description. Your widget can be war, criminal investigations, selling copiers, being a parent or spouse, caregiving, trading on the stock market, or making deli sandwiches. It doesn't matter what your job title is. How you behave, however, is a different matter altogether and is the thing that will define your culture.

You may be thinking to yourself that your team already has a culture established. Maybe you believe you have established a culture of *trust*. Or maybe the culture you believe you have established is one of *excellence*. You may or may not be right. I can't know if you are right until I hear from you about *how* you have established trust or excellence. What are the things you and your team *do* that create trust and excellence? You see, trust and excellence are merely by-products of what you do. They are the label you put on the result of the things you do and how you behave.

For example, imagine you were to approach me and tell me that I need to trust you because we will now trust each other to create a safe and predictable environment. My response may be, very reasonably, that I *don't* trust you. What's more, you can't simply make me trust you by telling me to trust you. Your reply may be something to the effect of, "Why don't you trust me?" My answer will likely consist of a list of the things that you *do* that make me not trust you. Now, as a leader, you must go about the business of *doing* certain things, or *not doing* certain things, to create the trust you want from me.

The same holds true for defining your culture with terms like "excellence." Please don't misunderstand—there is nothing wrong with saying things like, "We have a culture of excellence." My point is simply that most leaders who say this begin and end there. My question, again, will be *how* are you excellent? Excellence is the by-product of what you do and how you behave.

Let's break it down more simply. I ask, "Do you trust that person?"

You answer, "Yes."

I respond, "Why?"

You reply, "Because they pay attention when I talk to them. They always do what they say they are going to do. I can always count on them to tell me the truth."

Once again, I comment, "Your team's performance was excellent. I want that for my team. How did you do that?"

You answer, "We always plan before we act. We always finish what we start before moving on to other projects. We do not tolerate gossip or bad-mouthing. We do not make emotional decisions. Because we behave in these ways, we achieve excellence."

Using the Leadership Data

As we begin to understand how to establish good Guidelines for Behavior, let's talk about data. Leadership has long been thought of as an intangible behavior, one where leadership training can't really produce a definable return on investment. You may be surprised to learn that leadership studies have been around for some time. It's been my experience that organizations talk a big game on leadership but then use the excuse of return on investment, or the inability to track return on investment, as the excuse not to invest in leadership training. The investment I'm talking about is time, not money. Money is the excuse, but time is really the thing to which organizations don't want to commit. A commitment to time is what will ultimately bring the behavioral leadership change everyone is looking for.

There are enough studies to know that the financial cost of bad leadership can be crippling. For example, research conducted by the Blanchard Company shows that less-than-optimal leadership practices cost the typical organization an amount equal to as much as 7% of their total annual sales.[54] Sibson and Company estimate that employee turnover can result in a 16–50% cost as a percent of industry earnings.[55] The Saratoga Institute estimates that between 9% and 32% of that cost is directly attributable to poor management

54   Cullen, Susan. "Why Leadership Training Is Essential in Your Organization." Quantum Learning Solutions, Inc, October 2, 2017. https://www.quantumlearn.com/blog/why-leadership-training-is-essential-in-your-organization.

55   Witt, David. "The High Cost of Doing Nothing: Quantifying the Impact of Leadership on the Bottom Line." The Ken Blanchard Companies, December 10, 2009. https://leaderchat.org/2009/12/10/leadership-development-the-high-cost-of-doing-nothing-understanding-the-financial-impact/.

practices.[56] Meanwhile, the Blanchard Company estimates 30% of an annual salary to replace a lower-skilled, entry-level employee, to as much as 250% of an annual salary to replace a highly specialized or difficult-to-replace position.[57] For its part, the Saratoga Institute uses a 100% replacement cost for its calculations.[58]

It's not hard to understand that people leave their jobs because of bad leadership, and it costs a lot of money to replace them. It simply begs the question of what to do about it. How do organizations fix this problem? The studies of what makes great teams give us the answer or, at least, the start of the answer. A client of mine did an analysis of the financial output of employees who participated in consistent leadership training versus those who did not. The financial results of those who participated were significantly better than those who did not.

There have been a number of unrelated studies since the 1990s that have focused on what makes a great team: in 1995, David Lyle (et al.), "Leadership, Cohesion, and Team Norms Regarding Cheating and Aggression"; in 1999, Amy Edmundson, "Psychological Safety and Learning Behavior in Work Teams"; in 2010, Anita Williams Wooley (et al.), "Evidence for a Collective Intelligence Factor in the Performance of

---

56   Ibid.

57   Witt, David. "The High Cost of Doing Nothing: Quantifying the Impact of Leadership on the Bottom Line." The Ken Blanchard Companies, December 10, 2009. https://leaderchat.org/2009/12/10/leadership-development-the-high-cost-of-doing-nothing-understanding-the-financial-impact/.

58   Ibid.

Human Groups"; Google's "Project Aristotle" in 2015.[59] The key takeaway from all of these studies, at least from my perspective, was that great teams were established because of *how* they functioned, not *who* was on them.[60] Furthermore, the *how* was made up of behaviors, not things like having a to-do list, intelligence, or love of a job. And finally, the *how* needed to be established and enforced by the *leader*.[61]

So, since some very committed people went about the work of validating that behaviors make great teams and these behaviors are established and enforced by the leader, let's do them the courtesy of starting the discussion of what makes a good Guideline for Behavior with some of the studies' conclusions. But first, remember: *If we didn't change the way we made, marketed, or sold our widget, but behaved in* **these** *ways, would we get better?*

There are surprisingly only a couple of consistent behaviors that successful teams exhibit:

1. Everyone feels like they can speak up, and teammates speak in roughly the same proportion. Honest discussion can occur without fear of retribution or insult.

2. Teammates are sensitive to each other's emotions and needs. [62]

---

59   Duhigg, Charles. *Smarter Faster Better*. 1st ed. New York, NY: Random House, 2016.

60   Ibid.

61   Ibid.

62   Ibid.

In one of the studies, these behaviors were labeled "The Psychological Safe Zone."[63] According to the data, behave in these ways, and you will have a successful team. So, as you begin to understand the concept of Guidelines for Behavior inside the leadership process and search for where to start defining them for your team, family, or organization, perhaps the Psychological Safe Zone is a good place to begin.

I recognize I just summarized years' worth of studies in a few paragraphs. The goal of citing the studies is not to fully break them down. That's been done, and I encourage you to go read the studies yourself. The goal is to show how Guidelines for Behavior are the key to establishing a culture in which you can hold your team or organization accountable. Behave in these ways, and we will get better!

Breaking Down the Behaviors in the Psychological Safe Zone

Let's briefly break down why the behaviors in the Psychological Safe Zone will make your team better if the leader establishes them and enforces them, if it's not already painfully obvious to you. Recognize that these behaviors have nothing to do with your *widget*.

Everyone feels like they can speak up, and teammates speak in roughly the same proportion. Honest discussion can occur

---

63   Ibid.

without fear of retribution or insult. People don't speak up for many reasons. Shyness or a general fear of speaking up in a group are common reasons. This is where *teammates speak in roughly the same proportion* comes in.

Studies show that in a typical four-person group, two people will do 62% of the talking. In a six-person group, three people will do 70% of the talking; and in an eight-person group, three people will do 70% of the talking.[64] We all know these people. Perhaps you are that person? In any event, when we allow for so few people to dominate so much of a conversation, we are only getting the views, opinions, and ideas of those few people. Over time, people generally are not interested in fighting for speaking time in a meeting. It eventually will come down to an attitude of, "Just get me through this meeting so I can get out of here with some sanity."

People will *feel* like they can speak up when speaking up is a behavioral guideline. When people speak up, new ideas are generated and old ways of doing things are tweaked, adjusted, or thrown out. When people speak up, they feel like their opinion matters, and they have more skin in the conversation because they spoke up. As it turns out, according to one study cited, it seems people don't necessarily care too much if their idea is used. They just want to know it was heard.[65]

---

64   Thompson, Leigh. "How to Neutralize a Meeting Tyrant." Fortune, February 11, 2013. http://fortune.com/2013/02/11/how-to-neutralize-a-meeting-tyrant/.

65   Duhigg, Charles. *Smarter Faster Better.* 1st ed. New York, NY: Random House, 2016.

How do we stop two or three people from dominating 60–70% of the conversation? You, the leader, have to establish that *teammates speak in roughly the same proportion*; you, as the leader, get to respectfully enforce this guideline by politely interrupting your conversation hog by saying, "Bill, I'm sorry to interrupt you. Thank you for your input, but you know how we do business around here. We've only got an hour, and we need to hear from everyone. So, Jane, please weigh in on ..."

Remember from Chapter 13, if you can "reprimand" by saying, "That's not how we do business around here," and everyone understands, then you've established a good culture. In this case, *everyone feels like they can speak up* because it is how you do business. It is a behavioral guideline that represents how you do business. Because it's how you act, it is now a part of your culture.

Your conversation hog will never like it because, well, they are a conversation hog. But they will understand it and live by it because you, the leader, have established it and enforced the guideline.

Honest discussion can occur without fear of retribution or insult. This is the other reason people don't speak up—they don't feel like having people roll their eyes at them, talk behind their back, or snicker at them when they present an idea or an opinion. To form, it will probably be your conversation hog that does the eye-rolling, gossiping, or snickering when they don't have the floor. The leader's enforcement behind this one takes a little more courage, but if it's a behavioral guideline that makes us better, then it needs to be enforced.

A Quick Thought on Enforcement

How a leader enforces a guideline, especially one like this, comes down to personal style, or your ART. My personal style is very direct. I would probably address an eye roll or snicker in this way: "Ted, why are you rolling your eyes? That is not the way we do business around here. Before we move on, let me remind everyone how we behave. We operate in a Psychological Safe Zone, which means that people are free to talk without fear of retribution or insult. Any questions about that? Good. Phillip, please continue."

I hold Ted accountable by asking him why he rolled his eyes. He may or may not have a good answer. It doesn't matter because he was asked the question, and this confirms to my employees how we are doing business. The rest is a simple reminder to everyone of how important this guideline is to me. If the negative behavior continues and Ted has nothing but bad answers after he's been asked why, or held accountable, then we move to the consequence phase.

Is my way the correct way to handle this? Beats me. But it is how I would handle it. You may handle it with more subtlety, with a softer touch. Good! The bottom line is that, however you handle the situation, it should convey that this is not "how we do business here." We behave in *these* ways!

There is no sugar-coating it. Confrontation is difficult and will take many of you far outside your comfort zone. Unfortunately, it is a necessary evil because if you don't enforce this guideline, then it is no longer a guideline. It will become a behavior you tolerate, and it is that behavior that will define your team and you as a leader.

Emotional Sensitivity to Needs and Emotions

Teammates must be sensitive to each other's emotions and needs.

My intention for this book is for it to be a very clear and raw guide on the Ice Cold Leader Methodology—a user's manual, if you will. There are many stories behind the basis for my philosophies and leadership process. But, as you have hopefully seen, my intention is to bring the elements in their most raw form, not to regale you with the stories behind them. However, in the case of emotional sensitivity, I need to make an exception. The reason is simple: I can't come up with any other way to describe the importance of this element of the Psychological Safe Zone and how both elements work in conjunction with each other. Most importantly, if I can describe how emotional sensitivity can be applied on the battlefield, then you will surely see it can be applied to the board room and, most importantly, to our personal lives as leaders.

The following story will not focus on the elements of the combat but the principles of the leadership process. The background is as follows: In 2010, as an FBI Special Agent, I was attached to an Army Ranger Regiment in Afghanistan where we saw extensive combat operations. My primary responsibility was to collaborate with an Afghan interpreter, who had courageously volunteered to work with U.S. forces on these dangerous missions, to lead battlefield interviews after targets had been secured.

All operations were "kill or capture." I highlight this point to make clear that these were not run-of-the-mill operations (in war, very few are). They specifically targeted individuals in leadership positions who had an incentive to avoid being captured and, as such, surrounded themselves with loyal people who had an incentive to avoid being captured or to prevent their leader from being captured. In short, we needed to do things correctly, or the most severe consequences could be realized, all of which are unacceptable: mission failure, injury, or death.

Prior to each mission, the interpreter and I would discuss the target set to include the background of the target himself, any accomplices who may also be on target, the history of violence on the part of the target and accomplices, the presence of women and children on the target, and priorities depending on how much time we would have on target before we had to vacate, which could be anywhere from five minutes to one hour.

Just as how much time we would have on target varied, so too did the time we had for discussion prior to the operation, which could range, again, anywhere from only a few minutes to several hours.

Our strategies varied based on the priority of the target and very often around the cultural sensitivities at play (or, more specifically, the presence of women and children on the target). We would discuss the circumstances under which it would be appropriate to physically move women from one area of the target to another, even though that meant simply holding the arm of the woman while escorting them. If we decided we needed to interview a woman, how far away would we take them from their children? Would we take them out of view from everyone else on the target? Where and when would we search her person for weapons or explosives? What may be the consequences for that woman among her people after we leave the target because she was interviewed alone by Americans?

The interpreter would share what he felt were the cultural issues and potential consequences of deviating outside of cultural norms on the target, and we would both weigh these considerations against the importance of capturing or otherwise locating the actual target of the operation. While the final decision on our strategy was mine, we both expressed our opinions and ideas before every operation. All ideas were on the table and expressed freely, regardless of whether they were acted on. Our guideline: *Everyone feels like they can speak up, and teammates speak in roughly the same proportion. Honest discussion can occur without fear of retribution or insult.*

About an hour into a patrol one night, en route to our target location, our unit came under fire. We realized we were coming under friendly fire from a local Afghan Army unit. The patrol leader very quickly went about the business of sending all the standard non-verbal signals to relay to our Afghan partners that they were shooting at friendly forces. Unfortunately, these signals were to no avail. The patrol leader then called for the interpreter to come to his position. He was simply going to have the interpreter get on the megaphone and tell the Afghans to stop shooting, as we were a friendly American force. No one in our patrol fired back at the Afghan unit.

There was no immediate movement toward the patrol leader. Given my role, I assumed it was my job to find the interpreter and bring him over to the patrol leader. Here is where I make my very important caveat.

By this point, the incoming fire had become sporadic. I did not race through a hail of bullets to bring the interpreter to the patrol leader. People have done that and have been awarded appropriately for their bravery, selflessness, and heroism. That is not what I did. I did, however, have to run an adequate-enough distance to find the interpreter and bring him back to the patrol leader. It was not particularly heroic, but it was also not the most comfortable thing I have ever done. And this is the point ...

When I got to the interpreter, I quickly tapped him on the back to get his attention and told him, "Let's go." As I turned to run back to the patrol leader, I quickly realized I was alone. I turned back to the interpreter and said again, "C'mon, let's go!"

His response left no room for interpretation: "No."

That interpreter had come under fire many times before. He was as brave and selfless as they come. He had never exhib-ited anything other than bravery and professionalism on oper-ations. In that moment, however, he was just stuck. It doesn't matter why, and I never found out, or cared, why. But I had a decision to make.

I could have gone the macho, testosterone-fueled, impatient route and pulled him along while calling him names that questioned his manhood and courage. Alternatively, I could exercise a little psychological safety, understand that he was stuck in the moment due to temporary fear or some other emotion, and tell him, "It's OK. Trust me. It's OK." Which is what I did. He shook off whatever had him stuck, and we continued with a successful mission ... right after he got on the megaphone and told the Afghans to stop shooting at us, which they did.

I think this story breaks down the elements of the Psychological Safe Zone in a way that shows the research behind it is right on the mark and leaders at all levels should consider the Psychological Safe Zone as a Guideline for Behavior.

I've had leaders tell me they want to establish a culture of trust. The team needs to trust each other. As I outlined earlier, you can't just tell someone to trust you. They will not trust anyone just because they are directed that trust is now a part of the culture. The question we need to ask ourselves before we label an element of our desired culture, like trust, is, "What do we do to gain trust?"

The interpreter and I followed the guidelines for psychological safety to the letter. Each one of us was able to offer ideas to the other with the full knowledge that we would not be judged or laughed at. We both expressed our ideas fully and completely, neither one of us dominating the conversation. At a moment of urgency, I recognized his emotional state of mind and acted appropriately by assuring him that everything was OK and that he could trust me.

And he did trust me—not because I told him to but because I had earned his trust (and he mine) by consistently doing all the things the Psychological Safe Zone called for.

We established a culture by exercising psychological safety. What was the label we put on it? I have no idea because we never labeled it. For the sake of argument, let's call it a culture of trust. But we can call it trust only because of the things we did, our Guidelines for Behavior, not because we told each other that we needed to have trust. It simply does not work that way. What we DID established the trust.

You will also notice that the Psychological Safe Zone is not specific to combat. Yet, behaving in this way made us better warriors.

The point of discussing all the research on what makes great teams and of focusing on the Psychological Safe Zone is to establish a starting point for you, the leader, on Guidelines for Behavior. Another important thing to remember when it comes to Guidelines for Behavior is that no good behavior operates in a bubble. If you exercise a positive behavior, it will have positive and impactful ripple effects into other areas of your life and organization—so, too, will negative behaviors.

Make Them Your Own— How to Define and Practice Guidelines for Behavior

GUIDELINES FOR BEHAVIOR ARE ESSENTIAL TO ANY GREAT leader, team, organization, or family. They establish what you will hold people accountable for. They move teams past the grind of industry best practices to a predictable behavioral environment that people love and will thrive in, regardless of profession or circumstance.

The work for establishing your Guidelines for Behavior comes from Elements One and Two of the leadership process: Emotional Awareness and Recognition and Cultural Awareness and Recognition. We cannot establish good behavioral guidelines if we are not first aware of what is actually happening to us and around us. Being aware of our emotions and the actions they drive, without judgment and for better or worse, will allow us to identify areas for improvement. It will allow us to establish what we will hold ourselves and the people we lead accountable for.

If you are struggling to define your behaviors, do your research. If you are reading this book, you have probably read others like it that perhaps outline some leadership traits and behaviors that you like or are drawn toward. Try them out within the Guidelines for Behavior.

Remember, there are no absolutes. Guidelines for Behavior will be specific to you, the leader. They will reflect the needs of the organization and your personal behavioral compass.

Guidelines for Behavior are essential to the leadership process. However, choosing which Guidelines for Behavior are the right ones for you or your team requires some work. Welcome to the Art of Establishing Guidelines for Behavior. Some of your guidelines will remain forever because no matter how good you become at them, they are the bedrock for how you do business. That's fine! As you fine-tune guidelines, you may find that some can be retired because they were simple behaviors that have become ingrained, and you are ready to move on to more advanced ones.

Unfortunately, sometimes your messages will get misinterpreted. Sometimes accidentally, sometimes on purpose. Either way, the messaging is your responsibility because you delivered it. You either delivered the message with clarity or with ambiguity. If you're not sure what I mean, ask yourself if your Guideline for Behavior can be interpreted any other way than how you meant it. Put yourself in the shoes of "that guy," the lowest common denominator who is always looking for a way around things. Keep this concept in the back of your mind as we move on to some other examples of Guidelines for Behavior. We'll come back to this.

To this day, one of the best leaders I ever encountered was my commanding officer at SEAL Team 1. One of the many reasons was that he introduced me to the concept of Guidelines for Behavior. He laid out a series of short and very specific guidelines that he wanted his platoon leaders to abide by. If something went wrong, he could be counted on to bring you back to his guidelines for ... guidance. They were behavioral guidelines that we were always accountable for.

Over the years, I used many of his guidelines for myself as a leader and began to incorporate my own as I got the hang of what Guidelines for Behavior were all about. What I ended up with was my own version of Guidelines for Behavior. At the time, these guidelines were primarily based on my experiences, both good and bad, as both a surface warfare officer (ship driver) and special warfare officer (SEAL). They also included experiences during my time in the private sector and at the United States Naval Academy. The following are the verbatim Guidelines for Behavior I presented to my first sales team in the private sector, circa 2000. As I look back on them, I'm forced to smile. Not because I don't believe in them—I do. I might have, however, used a slightly gentler touch, beginning with the name. Or maybe I wouldn't have ...

Rules Set in Stone

I am a firm believer in guidelines and having a process in place to model how things should be done. I am also a firm believer that guidelines are just that: guidelines. They provide a road map that gives a general direction, not a course and speed that cannot be deviated from.

Having said that, I do have some rules that are set in stone and provide very little room for negotiation if violated.

1. **Be where you're supposed to be when you're supposed to be there.** If you are going to be late, call. If you don't know where you're supposed to be, call. If you make a call and tell me you are going to be late, I will not ask you why. If it becomes a pattern, we will have a discussion and fix the problem

2. **Pay attention to what is being discussed.** There is no greater inconsideration than having a sidebar conversation while someone else is talking. If you have something so important to say while someone else is speaking, politely interrupt and make your point. Being rude or appearing disinterested in what is being said is not something you would do with your customers, so I expect it will not be done with your teammates.

3. **Sell to the best of your ability.** I fully expect everyone to have an active life outside of (company name). However, during working hours, I expect all energy to be devoted to selling and making money. You will always be afforded the flexibility that comes with being a salesperson. That's one of the reasons we got into this business. That flexibility does not extend to excessive smoke breaks, an abundance of personal calls, or general inactivity in the office. Those types of activities do

not translate into selling to the best of your ability. If, from time to time, you have things to take care of and can only work half a day, fine. But work for half a day

4. **Never lie or be deceitful.** I expect mistakes. I expect bad things to happen. I even expect some dumb things to happen. Just tell me the truth about these things so they can be fixed immediately and we can move on. My passion for this cannot be overstated. Of all the rules stated, the most dire consequences come with violating this one.

With the exception of these rules, no two people will be treated the same. No two people are the same, so common sense dictates that no two people should be treated the same. If I am kept abreast of developments in your account, if you are following the process and you are making sales, you can be confident I will stay out of your way. If you are not doing these things, well ...

The Approach, Fallout, and Effect

Let's break these down first in the context of my approach. I let my boss review these before I sent them to my team. He approved. I was relocating from Washington, D.C., to New York City, so I emailed my guidelines (or, "Rules Set in Stone"), to my new team for review prior to meeting them for the first time. My intention was to set the expectations early and give everyone a chance to digest them. I wasn't blind to how these guidelines would come across to my new team as such clarity and straight-forwardness is usually reserved for military discussion.

About a day after I sent them to the team, I got a call from my boss. He advised me that the team was not happy, and I could expect mutiny when I arrived. I was a little surprised—not so much at the team's reaction (although "mutiny" seemed a little strong) but at my boss' delivery of the message. "I ran these by you before I sent them out. You said you were good with them," I said.

He responded, "I am. I love them. I just wanted to give you a heads-up as to what you are walking into. Good luck," he concluded with the subtlety of a sledgehammer.

I appreciated the heads-up and put together my plan for the initial meeting with my team. I believed in and trusted what I was doing so I had no concern about addressing the issue head-on and immediately. So I began, "Hello, my name is Errol. I'm happy to be your new manager. I understand there are some concerns with the document I sent everyone to review. Please address your concerns freely."

"Freely" was barely out of my mouth when the onslaught began.

"We're not your soldiers in the military!"

"How dare you treat us like children!"

"Are you calling us liars?"

"I've got ten years more sales experience than you have. What do you even know?"

I'm pretty sure there was a reference to Hitler in there as well.

After the initial salvo was complete, I asked, "Is that it?" I absorbed one or two more glancing blows, and then continued: "OK, I've heard everything you've said, and I understand how you feel. I'll make you a deal. Let's go over each one of these rules, and if you can make an argument as to why any of these behaviors should not be required, we will take them off. And, you don't even have to make a good argument. Just an argument."

Was my approach the right approach? I have no idea. If I had to do it today, I would probably make some adjustments to delivery and wording, specifically, with the word "rules." But what I believed in was the message, so I had no problem with defending the rules to a hostile crowd. I believed, based on my experience and personal beliefs, that even if we didn't change the explicit ways we made, marketed, or sold our widget, but changed our behaviors to align with my rules, we would get better as a sales team.

How does the story end? Happily! Of course, nobody could deny that it was better to be on time than late, for example. They just didn't like being told that. When I explained why these things were so important to me and what I saw when these things weren't done, the sales team started to understand and got on board. Furthermore, when I asked if anyone had ever seen these behaviors, or if things like gossiping made teams better, once again, everyone understood where I was coming from. I simply wanted to be clear about the behaviors for which I would be holding them accountable. By the end of the meeting, everyone was very comfortable with where we stood, and we went on to have a hugely successful team. Nothing was taken off the list.

Your approach to successfully delivering Guidelines for Behavior will come with experience. Unfortunately, there is no way around that fact. But how to deliver the message, and the message itself, are two different topics. We are focused on the message of Guidelines for Behavior. If you believe in the concept of Guidelines for Behavior, and you give thought to which Guidelines for Behavior are important to you, the leader, then your message will get through.

Another important element of good Guidelines for Behavior is that they are unambiguous. Guidelines for Behavior should be put in some context, even something as simple as "be on time." Ensure you clear up what "be on time" means to you. If you say, "We start at 9:00 a.m.," and someone dives through the door at exactly 9:00 a.m., are they on time? Or perhaps 9:00 a.m. means, "We will actually start the meeting at 9:00 a.m., so please be in your seats ready to go." These are small differences, but differences that need to be cleared up. However, the general guideline is clear and unambiguous. Nobody can turn it on its head to their benefit. For example, nobody can say, "Be on time? Oh, I thought you actually meant to be late." Remember "that guy" I referenced earlier? The one who will turn anything you say on its head to his (or her) benefit? Make your guidelines clear and unambiguous, with the necessary clarity and context provided, and you will have effectively and professionally neutralized your lowest common denominator.

Making Guidelines That Stick

Let's talk briefly about how to make your guidelines stick so you can make the simple reprimand everyone will understand: "That's not how we do business around here."

One thing that happens a lot is that leaders put out what they want from their teams once. Maybe they put it out in a document, and maybe they even have people sign the document. "We pledge to ..." and then nobody sees the document again, maybe ever. The leader might have actually identified Guidelines for Behavior in the document, but does this scenario meet with the spirit of what is trying to be achieved? Of course not. So, what to do?

If something is important enough to be said once, it is important enough to say over and over again. If you believe in Guidelines for Behavior and go about the business of identifying them, telling everyone one time what they are doing will not cut it. "OK, Errol, how often should we review them with our teams?"

The answer is simple: a lot!

Review however often it takes so you can eventually get to the one-sentence reprimand everyone will understand: "That's not how we do business around here."

Once a week? Yes. Once a month? Yes. Once a quarter? Yes. Every time a guideline is violated? Yes. Repeat it often enough so the Guideline for Behavior becomes part of your culture, the thing you do.

Best Practices Versus Guidelines for Behavior

The New York FBI SWAT Team was as good a combat team as I've ever been associated with. While SWAT was a collateral duty in the FBI, we trained regularly, and we trained hard. The overwhelming majority of our work was close-quarters battle (CQB). Essentially, CQB is the process of going into a house to arrest or locate a subject (bad guy). We were constantly honing and identifying CQB best practices, which are not to be mistaken for Guidelines for Behavior.

Best practices included things like how to enter a room properly and efficiently, how to clear a hallway, how to navigate a hallway intersection, and how to throw a flashbang into a room when the door is closed and when the door is open. Best practices seem to always change or be modified, which is good. This means you are always thinking about how to do your job better. On SWAT, we would drill the best practices until we had them down. Remember: *If you didn't change the way you make, market, or sell your widget, but behave in these ways, you will get better.*

Therefore, best practices don't fall under Guidelines for Behavior because they are specific to your widget (in this case, CQB). Our Guidelines for Behavior while conducting CQB were the constant. No matter what happened, if things were going badly, or we forgot how to execute a new best practice, we could always go back to our guidelines to get through a situation successfully. We had three guidelines for the New York SWAT Team:

- Read off the operator in front of you.
- Cover your buddy.
- Find work.

How often did we review these guidelines? Every time we practiced CQB. On a single day of training CQB, we might have gone through 50 to 100 practice runs. How often did we review the Guidelines for Behavior? Fifty to 100 times a day. Every critique of a best practice would inevitably fall under a Guideline for Behavior.

For example, let's say the best practice was for the first operator to enter a room and go to the left, the next operator to go right, and the third operator to go to the center. Now, let's say the first operator goes to the left, but the second operator goes to the center instead of the right. You, as the third operator, know that you are supposed to go to the center. So, what do you do? Well, the best practice says for you to go to the center, but if you go to the center, as per the best practice, you will leave the right side of the room uncovered and potentially put all your fellow operators at risk (because maybe the bad guy is hiding in the corner of the right side of the room with a gun!). You will be technically correct if you go to the center, but it is not the correct decision.

Remember, Guidelines for Behavior bring us back on track when things are going wrong. In this instance, things went wrong as soon as the second operator went to the center of the room instead of the right side of the room. So, as the third operator, you go back to your Guidelines for Behavior that have been drilled into your brain in what seems like an endless fashion. But now, you realize why. You, as the third operator, immediately go to them for answers. In this case, you can pick one of two behaviors that will fix the situation.

Read off the operator in front of you. The number two operator went to the center instead of the right. Therefore, I will read off their movement and go to the right. The number three operator has just avoided a potentially life-threatening situation by following a simple guideline for behavior. Common sense? Yes. Common practice? No! Simply stated, I've seen countless number three operators go to the center even though the number two operator was already there.

Cover your buddy. This behavior will net the same result but with a different thought process. Using the same scenario, the number three operator simply identifies that the right side of the room is not covered by anyone. Further, the number three operator knows that there could potentially be a threat on the right side of the room that could have devastating results on their teammates. (Remember the bad guy!) So, the number three operator goes to the right to cover his buddy.

For the sake of thoroughness, let's look at another example for the last guideline: find work. When conducting CQB, operators generally form a single line as they move through the house. The operators who get caught toward the end of the line don't always get much action, i.e., room entries. That's just the way it goes sometimes. What happens sometimes is that the operators at the end of the line may tend to lose a little focus. The third guideline will ensure that this does not happen.

If the operators toward the end of the line are trying to find work, guess what they are not doing? Staring at the head of the operator in front of them waiting for their turn to enter a room and potentially losing focus. Instead, they notice a chair or table that may inhibit movement toward the next room. So, they jump out of the line, move the obstacle, and get back in line. Or, they notice one of the operators in the front of the line may need a flashbang to enter a room, and they don't appear to have one. So, they jump out of line, give the operator their flashbang, and get back in line.

The point is, there is usually something you can be doing. If you have not actually found work, then you are always actively looking. This keeps you focused and, more importantly, assists the overall efficiency of the operation. "Find work" is not specific to CQB, but it makes the SWAT team better at CQB. Therefore, it is a great example of a Guideline for Behavior.

How It Works at Home

My premise has been that the Ice Cold Leader Methodology is applicable to every aspect of life: combat, business, and your personal life at home. We've covered business and combat, so let's talk about the home.

New Year's is a time of great hope and new beginnings. Every year we try to make positive adjustments to our life. We put forward a list of very specific goals and actions we are going to take to achieve those goals. This is all good! I'm not about to suggest that new beginnings, goals, and actions aren't positive. What I am going to suggest, however, is that perhaps, we generally go about it all wrong. I think we tend to focus too much on the specific actions—or best practices, if you will—when we should focus instead on Guidelines for Behavior.

My family is no different. This past New Year's, my wife and I sat down to look for common areas of growth together. We immediately focused on the master bedroom and bathroom. As we were embarrassed to admit, we were trending backward and occasionally resembled teenagers in the way we straightened up and cleaned our bedroom and bathroom. Three small children, three dogs, and two working parents will do that to you if you let it. Guests were not going to stroll into our bedroom, so best to focus cleaning on the kitchen, family room, living room, and anywhere else a guest may roam. But enough was enough, and it was time to act like adults and set the right example for our children. Our bedroom and bathroom would be the cleanest parts of the house! (Did I mention how embarrassing this is?)

We resolved to deep clean the bedroom and bathroom once a week. We made a list of what would be cleaned when and who was responsible. All good, right? We set a specific goal and identified actions.

But something felt wrong with the process. Yes, we needed to be tidier, but was this really something that was going to make us better all around? Wasn't there a behavior that would cover tidying up the master bedroom but also benefit other areas of our life? Is this really what our life's goals had come down to? "Clean the toilet" as a New Year's resolution?

Read off the operator in front of you, cover your buddy, find work. YES! These were behaviors we could apply, or commit to, that would make us better without focusing on just cleaning the toilet! We ended up combining all three into one behavior, but all three were in play. So, what does this look like?

If my wife is cleaning the dishes, I grab the garbage. If my wife is dressing our son for school, I make sure our daughter is eating her breakfast. If I am getting frustrated helping our son with his homework, my wife steps in and gives me a break so he gets the attention and positive energy he needs.

What else? Find work. I have a couple of minutes to spare and pass by that stack of mail on the counter. (Yes, you know that stack of mail!) I grab a handful and clear it out. I'm brushing my teeth and notice the counter is getting a little crusty. I grab a Clorox wipe and wipe it down while I'm brushing my teeth. Dishes are stacking up, but I don't have time to do them all. But, I have time to do a few, so I do a few. I've found fifteen minutes! Instead of turning on a mindless television show or randomly surfing the web, I remember we have three dogs and go clean as much of the yard as I can.

You get it. When we focus on the behavior, a lot of different things get done that very soon make life easier and more orderly.

How about this for finding work? My daughter has had a rough day and isn't her normal happy-go-lucky self. My wife puts down everything she is doing and sits with her for a little while to comfort her and show her the love she clearly needs. How do we recognize found work? We go back to Chapter 15 and remember that, as leaders, we are always in the moment and aware of what is happening to us and around us. Because we are in the moment and aware, we can identify what either needs to be done or can be done. Because we are in the moment, we can step outside ourselves and find work.

Implementing Your Guidelines for Behavior

I LOVED BEING A SPECIAL AGENT FOR THE FBI. SOME OF THE greatest leaders I have ever met sat in the FBI offices in New York City and led amazing cases that had a profound impact in New York City, the United States, and around the world. However, as I've stated many times, my opinion is that those great leaders in the FBI I am speaking of were outliers, not the norm.

I bring this up not to take a gratuitous shot at the FBI. I bring it up to highlight that, despite loving the job of FBI Special Agent, the environment drove me away. As I spent time in New York City, I would see consistent flashes of poor leadership that I had a hard time believing were really happening—half-truths, lies, jealousy, vindictiveness, "my way or the highway," laziness, outsized and misplaced ego, gossip, and pettiness. It was hard to believe. But it wasn't until I left the New York Office and transferred to a much smaller office in a different state that I fully realized the overall corrosive environment I was a part of.

Every single Guideline for Behavior I cite in this section was not only lacking in that smaller office, but the culture also consisted of the opposite behaviors. Lateness to meetings and not paying attention or otherwise rude behaviors during meetings were the norm. Half-truths and innuendo were treated as fact (in some cases, so was outright lying). When an idea was put on the table for discussion, you could count on gossip, bad-mouthing, and mean-spiritedness to follow. A few people forcefully and rudely dominated the conversation.

Here's the really disturbing thing: that behavior was prevalent in only a small handful of people. Yet, it prevailed and poisoned the overall culture and morale of the office. Why and how? I watched "leader" after "leader" come through that office and tolerate the anti-social and unprofessional behavior of a few. Because the "leaders" tolerated, and in many instances took part in, the behavior I described, it became the fabric and reputation of the office.

It didn't matter that the vast majority of the people in the office were good people. They were forced to accept the wholly objectionable behavior of a few because it was tolerated and often promulgated by "leadership."

What's my point here? It is to reiterate that leaders set the tone for behavior. A few people of bad intention and character can poison an entire team if left unchecked by one person. The team can fight these people and marginalize them but only if their resolve to fight is matched by the leader. Otherwise, negativity will prevail.

I loved being a Navy SEAL because of both the job and the environment created by the great people and leaders of the SEAL Team community. I loved being a copier salesman because of the safe and predictable environment that was created by the leader—not because I loved selling copiers. I loved doing the work of an FBI Special Agent. But the environment and the prevalent behaviors inside the FBI put me in the position to decide to stay or leave. So, I left.

My position is that leaders should focus on creating an environment people love and that an environment people love is one that is predictable. Remember one of the examples I gave previously: If the leader treats you one way today and another way tomorrow, that's an unpredictable environment people will grow tired of. If teammates can vent, criticize, and demean at the whim of their emotions without having to answer to the leader for their behavior ... that's an unpredictable environment people will grow tired of.

Where to Start

I understand that if you are reading this book, you may be in the middle of a difficult situation like I described at the FBI. So, what to do? How and where do you start the process of turning things around? Well, the only good place to start anything is the place you actually start. Don't wait for the perfect opportunity or for things to slow down. There is no perfect opportunity, and things won't slow down. Understand this as a fact, and it will be easier to start. There is no wrong time to begin positive change.

That said, how you implement what you believe is, again, different from what you believe. You must first work to understand the principle behind Guidelines for Behavior.

If we didn't change the way we made, marketed, or sold our widget, but behaved in these ways, would we get better?

Identify one or two behaviors, and ask yourself at the end of each day if you did them. Steal a couple from my examples, and take them for a test drive. Ask yourself at the end of each day if you "found work" or "finished what you started." Be conscious, or in the moment, as to their impact on your personal and professional life. Then try some others. Be on time, listen, don't gossip or bad-mouth, etc., and be conscious of their impact on your personal and professional life.

The next challenge is to implement them in your team. I'm not hiding or running away from the fact that this will be difficult. It will. Welcome to leadership! I can't tell you how to do it because I'm not you. How I do it may not work for you because we are two different people. You will have to experiment. You will have to see what works for you and what doesn't. You will have to summon the courage to fail, adjust, fail a little less, adjust, and continue to rinse and repeat until you have found your formula. I can, however, offer a couple of suggestions to get you started.

How to Get Your Team Started

Begin with one guideline—a simple one that everyone gets and that you can easily begin doing. "Be on time" or "pay attention" are easy ones that will begin the process. Nobody will look at you sideways if you begin saying that you expect everyone to be on time and pay attention. Why? Because everyone will agree with you! Now, just because they agree with you does not mean they will obey you. Strange, but true. We'll cover this in "The Resistance."

You may or may not give an explanation for your new guidelines. Again, experience will give you this answer. But, begin mentioning the behavior out loud, and you are making it clear that people are now answerable, or accountable, for that behavior. Besides getting people to be on time and paying attention, you are doing something else: you are beginning the process of setting Guidelines for Behavior. So, when you throw in another one, it will be less of a splash of cold water in everyone's face. You will have begun the process of making the behavioral environment predictable. You will have begun establishing what people are going to be held accountable for.

Perhaps you could go a little more formal. Perhaps you could begin with one or two of the simple behaviors, sit everyone down, and explain what is on your mind and why you are even bringing this up. Maybe it looks something like this:

> I want to address something that has been bothering me for some time. I'm sure I'm not the only one who notices that our meetings never really begin on time. First, let me say, it's my fault. For such a small behavior, I believe it has a negative impact on our overall performance and culture. When we are not on time, I believe it sends a message to everyone that we are not respectful of each other's time. And if we are not respectful of each other's time, it begs the question of

what else we are not respectful of regarding each other. I believe it chips away at fundamental trust. That said, I'd like all of us to be conscious of being on time. For me, that means if the meeting is scheduled to start at 9:00 a.m., everyone is seated and ready to begin at 9:00 a.m. For my part, I will not only abide by this but will also address lateness until being on time becomes a habit for our team. It's a small thing, but if we do it right and consistently, I believe it will have a positive impact.

Substitute "pay attention," "no gossip or bad-mouthing," or "no lies or half-truths" or "be on time" for the guideline of your choice. Imagine gradually incorporating each one after "be on time" has become a habit. This is an easy and effective way to begin, especially if you are in the middle of a bad situation. Take it one step at a time.

Perhaps these very basic behavioral guidelines don't apply to your team. Maybe you see room for improvement, but these basic behaviors are already in place. Fantastic! Then you can jump in with things like, "find work," or "we finish what we start", or "we look for answers before we ask questions." Navy SEAL ethos dictates things like "prioritize and execute," "decentralize command," and the need to keep things simple. These are excellent Guidelines for Behavior if you already have a team that is operating at a high level but still has room for growth.

Implementing Guidelines for Behavior toes a fine line between being aggressive and being patient. You see that they are important, and you are anxious to begin implementing them. Good! However, you also know that hitting everyone over the head with them may not be the best approach. So, don't. Be aggressive but patient. Be consistent but not overbearing.

Consistency and clarity will get you there. You may be worried that you'll come across as inauthentic or hypocritical because you're always late. Nothing is more authentic than honestly admitting a fault and deciding you are going to work to improve it.

So, when you hear, "What's up, Errol? Suddenly you are telling us how to act and what to do? You're never on time! A bit hypocritical, don't you think?"

Your response to this is simple because it's true: "I know. And it's a bad behavior that has a negative impact on everyone. That is why I'm going to change it in myself and ask the same of the team. I want to get better. I want our team to get better. I can't change how I acted in the past, but I can change this behavior going forward."

What's important is that you believe in the message, and you do your best to deliver it positively in a way that fits your personality. Again, it will be difficult if you are in the middle of a tough situation. Trust in this process, though. It will begin to create the environment people love to be a part of.

Too Many Is None

There is no need to pile on Guidelines for Behavior. One to three behaviors will do the trick because good behavior does not operate in a bubble. It will have positive effects outside the behavior itself. Imagine if you and/or your team performed the following behaviors flawlessly: prioritize and execute to completion, plan before we act, operate in a Psychological Safe Zone. (Remember the research?) If you did these three things well, would you get better? Would you get significantly better? Yes, you would. One to three is plenty!

So, let's break down the leadership process to this point. Emotions drive our actions. We must be situationally aware of our emotions in order to drive the actions we want. Culture is made up of the things you do, not the labels you put on them. Just like our emotions, we must be situationally aware of the things we and those around us do to identify our current culture. Once you identify what you and those around you do that make up your current culture, you are in a position to define what you want to do, or how you want to behave, by identifying Guidelines for Behavior.

Now you, the leader, are establishing what you and your team do that makes up your culture as well as what you will hold people accountable for.

Practicing the Art

Once you've established what you want for your Guidelines for Behavior, the real challenge will come with implementing them. No matter how you decide to implement them, doing so will take one overwhelming characteristic: courage.

Before we step into an ice bath, we do certain things to prepare. We breathe to obtain a mental and emotional focus as well as dull our pain receptors. When we are in the ice bath, we are in the moment and focused on our breath to remain calm amidst the chaos the ice bath represents. When we exit the ice bath, we maintain focus and begin the process of warming ourselves in a controlled fashion by way of an exercise called the horse stance. There is only one place where process is not a part of the equation: when we decide to step into the ice bath.

As much as you prepare to get in, you still must decide. You still must summon the courage to do something your every instinct is telling you not to, even though you know the benefits will be massive and long-lasting. You will either act with courage and get in or act with cowardice and not get in.

Now, relax. I'm not challenging your ego here with the word "cowardice," and I'm not calling you a coward. However, the simple fact remains that if you make the decision to get in the ice bath, it is a courageous one. If you make the decision not to get in, it is the opposite of courage ... cowardice.

By consistently stepping into the ice bath, day after day, week after week, and year after year, you are conditioning your brain to make courageous decisions. You are building a habit. You are creating a Guideline for Behavior that will pave the way to implement your personal or team Guidelines for Behavior: "I act with courage." Does it meet the test? If you act with courage in your decision-making process, will you get better? I think yes.

If you act with courage and implement your Guidelines for Behavior at work, at home, or in your personal life, will you get better? Yes!

You must practice anything to be good at it. Courage is no different. Stepping into an ice bath will help you practice making courageous decisions because implementing your Guidelines for Behavior will take courage.

Courage is just one example of a behavioral guideline you can practice by practicing cold exposure. Think about the cold exposure drill you did during Cultural Awareness and Recognition. What did you observe about yourself before stepping into an ice bath or cold shower? Did you procrastinate? Did you make excuses to not get in? Did you not turn the shower all the way to cold? Did you hoot and holler when you got in and over-dramatize the entire experience?

Choose a Behavior and Provide Context

Now decide how you want to behave in the cold. You may decide you want to act like a professional. Acting like a professional may mean something a little different to all of us, so it is important to identify what it means to you. Perhaps to you, it means not overreacting to an external stimulus, like the cold ... or that co-worker. Now you have a clear idea of what the behavior looks like and can go about working on it.

You now know what the effect of focusing on one thing has on your brain and what focusing on your breath and ensuring a conscious exhale has on your nervous system. It calms you down. So, with that in mind, you enter the ice bath, recognize the fight-or-flight effects of the cold, and focus on your breath. When all the external factors that the cold will drive you toward come to the surface (Get me out of here! It's too cold! How much longer? I hate this! I can't do this anymore!), you acknowledge them and move your focus back to your breath. No matter how many times your mind wanders, you bring it back to your breath.

Soon enough, you will be entering and remaining in the cold like a professional. No overly dramatic displays of emotion. No excuses or focus on external environmental factors. Just focus and calm, like a professional.

Context is vital to behavioral guidelines and will allow you to focus and act with intention. Maybe defining the behavior as acting like a professional doesn't work for you. However, you like the idea of recognizing your emotions and focusing on your breath as behaviors. That's fine—these are still behaviors, and they mean more to you than the idea of acting like a professional, so go with those.

This is why cold exposure is vital to practicing the Art of Guidelines for Behavior. It will allow you to define exactly the behavior you want to work on as an individual. When you are able to provide that focus for your own personal behaviors, you will be in a much better position to identify them for your team. You will be able to display empathy for and understanding of what needs change. Then, you will be able to put into context the necessary behaviors to create the culture you want for your team by identifying what behaviors you will be holding your team accountable for.

When Everything Stays the Same, Nothing Changes

Back in the 1900s, scientists conducted a study on rodents to see if new neurons could grow in the brain. The scientists concluded it was not possible. It appeared we were doomed to our current state of brain function.[66]

Later, however, the study of neurogenesis told us this was inaccurate. In fact, the brain can grow new neurons. When you learn new things and have new experiences you make new connections and grow new neurons.[67,68] It's called neuroplasticity, the brain's ability to reorganize itself by forming new neural connections throughout life. Neuroplasticity allows neurons to adjust their activities in response to new situations or changes in the environment. In other words, the brain can rewire itself and grow new neurons when it's stimulated by new things or experiences.[69,70]

So, what was wrong with the rodent study where scientists concluded that the brain could not produce new neurons? The rodent's environment never changed. So, because their

---

66   *Rewired: Introduction To Your Brain.* Gaia Network, 2019. https://www.gaia.com/series/rewired.

67   Ibid.

68   Dispenza, Dr. Joe. *Becoming Supernatural: How Common People Are Doing the Uncommon.* 2nd ed. Carlsbad, CA: Hay House, 2019.

69   Doidge, Norman. *The Brain That Changes Itself: Stories of Personal Triumph from the Frontiers of Brain Science.* 1st ed. New York, NY: Penguin Group, 2007.

70   *Rewired: Introduction To Your Brain.* Gaia Network, 2019. https://www.gaia.com/series/rewired.

environment never changed, they had no new thoughts or experiences, so their brains stayed the same.[71]

Remember what the research said about our thoughts, emotions, and the mind/body connection? Now we know that when everything stays the same, nothing changes. And we further know that very little of what we do or think changes. And we wonder why we can't make positive change in our lives when we think and do the same things over and over!

If You Change Things, Things Will Change

TRIGGER to EMOTION to THINK/DECIDE to ACT. Your new behavioral guidelines are the first things you should think about inside of "THINK/DECIDE." You have done the hard work of observing your current culture or what you do. In exercising the Art of Guidelines for Behavior you identified what you want to do or how you want to behave. You have exercised courage in your decision-making, perhaps. When you did that, you experienced something new and created a new emotion. The results were likely good because we moved away from those emotions and actions of stress.

Perhaps you behaved with patience, empathy, gratitude, grace, or love as part of your new behaviors. Maybe you focused on finding your breath during stressful times. Maybe you prioritized and executed to completion. Maybe you found

---

71   *Rewired: Introduction To Your Brain.* Gaia Network, 2019. https://www.gaia.com/series/rewired.

work or covered your buddy or planned before you acted. Regardless, you moved to conscious action that is positive.

When you did this, the neurons in your brain began to form new networks, and the brain began to make new chemicals to replace the ragged, tired, and destructive chemicals produced by your previous negative behaviors and emotions of stress. Then, you did it over and over, and the new neural pathways in your brain became stronger and stronger as the old ones faded away because they were not being used anymore.

Now, you are acting with courage or grace or love or gratitude or focus. The more you act with it, the more you become it, and eventually, it becomes your personality. It has become what you do because you have literally changed your mindset by simply identifying a positive behavior that produces new experiences and new emotions. You are no longer the rat in an unchanging environment who never changes and wonders why.

I'm not sure I can paint with any broader brush when it comes to this portion of the science. But it should give you what you need to appreciate and understand the impact the Ice Cold Leader Methodology will have on your life from a scientific standpoint. In short, to make changes, you must come out of your current, perhaps stagnant, state and make a decision about your current behavior and what you want to replace it with. You have to feel the impact of that decision because it must create an emotional experience greater than the one you are replacing it with.

Element Four—The Planning Process

WHEN WE MEET FAILURE IN OUR LIVES, WE BECOME VERY adept at assigning blame to outside forces. There wasn't enough time, people weren't committed, we didn't have the resources, alien invasion, or it just wasn't meant to be.

Here's the hard truth: Failure comes from one reason and one reason only ... bad planning. We fail because we don't cover the consistent and proven elements necessary to achieve success. The ones that give us the right questions to ask, allow our people to work with initiative and autonomy, or allow us to unemotionally prioritize and then methodically execute.

Each element of the leadership process builds on the one before it. We started with Emotional Awareness and Recognition because emotions drive our Actions. Then we moved to Cultural Awareness and Recognition because culture is the sum total of the Actions we take; those Actions ultimately make up our culture. And then, we identified what Actions we want to make up our culture, so we established Guidelines for Behavior that would begin the process of identifying what we would hold people accountable for.

The first three elements of the process allow the leader to create a predictable environment people will love to be a part of. But ultimately, leaders need to drive Mission accomplishment. And to drive Mission accomplishment, leaders need to plan with precision and discipline.

The Planning Process will be broken down into three chapters. This chapter will break down each element of the Planning Process in detail as a project management tool. The next chapters will go over how the Planning Process is used as a leadership tool and will cover things like how it helps prioritization, creates initiative, and allows you to work under pressure in a calm and methodical fashion.

Modified Navy SEAL Planning

Let's begin with the breakdown of the Planning Process. This process is a simplified and modified version of the process I learned and used as a Navy SEAL platoon commander. The reason I bring this up is because it serves as a reminder that the operations we conducted in the SEAL Teams tended to be dangerous, and if we didn't consciously account for each element of the Planning Process, we ran the risk of missing one. If we missed one of the elements, the chances of something going wrong increased exponentially. The something "going wrong" could mean one of three things: mission failure, injury, or death. All three of these are completely unacceptable, especially if they could be reasonably avoided by simply following the elements of the Planning Process.

The beauty of this process is that its effectiveness on the battlefield is 100% transferable to the boardroom and the kitchen table. It can be used for massive initiatives, the small fires that seem to plague us by the hour, or the internal struggles we face daily, both at work and at home.

The elements of the Planning Process form the acronym SMACCC, which stands for Situation, Mission, Actions, Contingencies, Command, and Communication. Now, let's go over each element and how to apply it.

SMACCC: "Situation"

The Situation is the set of background circumstances dictating a need for Action.

Why are you doing something, or why are you about to do something? To make it clearer, if you hear someone describe a scenario, and your response is, "Well, what are we doing about that?" or "We need to do something about that," then the Situation has been clearly identified because it specifically lays out the need for Action.

If your response is, "So what?" then you don't have a need for Action. You've just saved yourself and your team a lot of wasted time by clearly determining if a set of circumstances dictates a need for Action. The Situation is not always geared toward a problem. A set of circumstances dictating a need for Action can be an opportunity as well. The crux of the Situation is that if you fail to act on the given set of circumstances that require Action, it will have a negative impact on your work or life.

The Situation instills an overall sense of purpose. As the work trickles down to the line-level workers, they should always understand why they are doing something or be able to ask the leader why they are doing something and get a clear and concise answer.

The Situation must be defined by the leader. If the leader does not define the Situation, then work is getting done randomly and without purpose. Projects will die a quick death or take sharp drastic turns that seem to have no rhyme or reason simply because people don't know why they are doing what they are doing.

Teams often act on circumstances that they don't really need to act on, or at least not right then, because they have not first evaluated whether a set of circumstances will negatively impact their work if left unchecked. That evaluation helps determine the Actions that are necessary. Making sure you understand the circumstances and the potential negative impacts of Action and inaction will ensure you and your team are acting on things that really matter and will impact your organization, team, or family.

Think about those fires that plague you every day. If you've ever bothered to ask what the Situation was, or why you were asked to do that particular thing IMMEDIATELY, did you get a clear and concise answer that would allow you to properly prioritize that work because you understood the importance of it?

If you have asked for the Situation, how often was the answer akin to something like, "Well, Jan said it needed to be done," and it was left at that? So often we either don't ask the Situation, don't tell somebody the Situation, or nobody knows the Situation. Hence, we're not even sure why we are doing the work we are doing. But we do it. And then we have a million fires to contend with before we know it.

The Situation is the element of the Planning Process most frequently overlooked or under-communicated, perhaps because it takes a little extra effort to articulate why we want people to go in a particular direction. Yes, it does take more work up front to clearly identify and articulate the background circumstances that have led to the need for Action. But without the clarification, focus, efficiency, and purpose are lost, and results or Mission success suffer.

When you ask someone, "Why?" you are really just asking them to articulate the Situation. (Might this be a Guideline for Behavior to consider? Ask "Why?")

SMACCC: "Mission"

A Mission is simply your goal—*what you are specifically trying to achieve.*

You have identified your Situation or set of circumstances that determine a need for Action. If you have determined you need to act, then you need to act with a specific purpose, or you need to have a clearly defined Mission. Your Mission is what you're going to do about the Situation.

Whatever you want to accomplish needs to be clearly defined—everyone on your team needs to know exactly what the Mission is and exactly what you're trying to accomplish. Having a clearly-defined Mission sounds like common sense, and it is. But it's not always common practice. Disagreements on issues that seem to take a million different directions are often mitigated quickly when we can remind each other what we are specifically trying to accomplish, or what the Mission is.

If you are confused as to whether you or one of your people should do a certain thing or perform a certain task, all you have to do is ask yourself if that task gets you closer to accomplishing your Mission. If the task does get you closer to your Mission, then you have your answer. It's generally that simple. But, like the Situation, the Mission is not always clearly defined or articulated by the leader. Sometimes the Mission is unclear because several Missions have been identified as one big Mission. You may very well find you have several Missions that need to be accomplished. That's fine; simply break them out individually so they are clear.

The leader identifies the Situation and sets the Mission.

SMACCC: "Actions"

Actions are the steps that need to be accomplished to complete the Mission.

Along with identifying what Actions need to take place to accomplish the Mission, we also need to identify when those Actions will be completed. It doesn't matter how complex or simple the Actions are. If they are not identified, then they either won't get done, or you are hoping or assuming they will get done. Remember what we say about hope and assumptions: they have no place in the leadership process.

Identify the Actions that need to take place to accomplish the Mission. Identify when those Actions are to be completed.

Who should identify the Actions? We'll cover that in the Art of SMACCC. For now, as a leader, just know that Actions and when they will be completed need to be identified for an effective plan to take place.

SMACCC: "Command"

Command designates specific people to be responsible and accountable for completing specific Actions for the Mission.

If an Action needs to take place, then there needs to be a name next to it to clearly identify who is in charge of, or in Command of, that Action.

Once we clearly identify the Actions that need to take place to accomplish our Mission, Command needs to be assigned to those Actions. Once again, if we are not assigning Command next to an Action, then we are either hoping or assuming it will get done. Leaders don't hope and assume. They make clear who is in Command of getting each Action accomplished.

The same is true for the overall Mission. One person is in Command of the Mission. One person must be given authority to make decisions inside the clearly defined Mission. One person. Leadership by committee is no leadership at all.

Command is not, "I command you to do this!" Command is the act of assigning who is in charge of what.

This is where the company's organizational chart, or dotted lines of authority, get thrown out the window. Why? Because each Mission should have its own organizational chart. So, in the overall hierarchy of your organization, you and another person may be peers, so you've got no authority over them in the overall scheme and context of your organization. That's fine.

However, for a particular project, or Mission, when one person assumes Command then they have overall authority over that Mission regardless of what the company organizational chart says. This is why we need clearly defined Command for every Mission and every Action—it establishes final decision-making authority. Final decision-making authority inside a Mission is critical because, again, leadership by committee is no leadership at all.

Remember, we can't hold people accountable if they don't know what they are supposed to be accountable for. Inside the Planning Process, assigning Command makes it clear what people will be held accountable for, whether it's the overall Mission or each Action inside the Mission.

SMACCC: "Contingencies"

We must plan for the things that can go wrong by identifying Contingencies for each Action.

Contingencies are defined as "something that might possibly happen in the future, usually causing problems or making further arrangements necessary." When we identify Actions, we obviously feel like those Actions are the appropriate ones required to achieve our Mission. The reality, however, tells us that sometimes things go wrong. A good plan accounts for the things that can go wrong by identifying Contingency plans for each Action.

Look at each Action, and identify a couple of things that can go wrong, and then account for them. This concept is simple but can get tricky. How much time should we spend on how we will execute each Contingency? Does each Contingency require an entirely new plan? I can think of 100 things that can go wrong; we can't account for each one!

Planning for Contingencies will be the hardest thing you do. You will find there are either a million potential problems that come to mind or none at all. It takes practice and experience to get these right, so don't worry about perfection when you're just getting started. Start by at least thinking about them, and the Contingencies will find you. We will discuss some of the nuances of Contingencies in the next chapter. For now, it is important that you know to account for Contingencies. As long as you are constantly asking yourself, "What can go wrong with this Action?" you will quickly build your experience base and become increasingly adept at understanding the depth and detail you need to put into the Contingencies. Some Contingencies will be running Contingencies, meaning you will always be accounting for them. Some will be very specific.

Experience will be your guide. But to gain the necessary experience, you must always begin the process of accounting for Contingencies.

Let me share a couple of simple examples from both combat and business. My combat example is hardly exciting, but it highlights the importance of Contingency planning, even in the simplest of scenarios.

When I was a platoon commander in the SEAL Teams, I had just briefed my commanding officer on an operation. He approved the operation, which included when rehearsals were to be conducted before we left for the operation. Later in the day, I checked in with him to give him an update, and he asked me if rehearsals had been conducted. I replied that we had conducted rehearsals for the Actions on target.

Then he asked if we had rehearsed loading the helicopter. I was a bit confused, so I asked, "Excuse me?" He reiterated, "Have you rehearsed loading the helicopter?"

Still a bit confused, I inquired, "You want us to rehearse walking out to the helicopter and getting in?"

The conversation took a quick turn, "Lieutenant Doebler, if you feel rehearsing part of your insertion plan is beneath you, I'll happily find someone who does not feel that way and let them execute the Mission."

With that, I advised my commanding officer we would complete the rehearsal immediately.

What can go wrong walking out to the helicopter? I felt a little silly getting the platoon together to rehearse walking out to the helicopter. When I explained what we were doing, one of the more senior members of the platoon remarked that he had severely sprained his ankle jogging out to the helicopter years ago and had to miss the operation. And there it was. Now I understood why the commanding officer didn't extend a lot of his patience with me when I questioned him about rehearsing this. There were very basic things that could go wrong, and I wasn't accounting for them.

Well, what happens if someone turns their ankle and breaks it? It sounds like a silly thing to account for until it actually happens, and I haven't accounted for it. Sure, that person obviously isn't going on the operation, but what of the skill set we've just lost? What if that operator was a sniper? Do I have another sniper going on the operation? Is the operation contingent upon sniper support? Can we conduct the operation with just one sniper team ... or no sniper teams?

Because I accounted for the potential (if, however, unlikely) loss of a key element of the operation, we were in a position to move forward without delay. In this case, we built in some redundancy of personnel and skill set. We were able to devise a scenario to accomplish the Mission with limited resources, or we could put this in as a "no-go" criterion. In other words, if this happens, the operation is off.

It may be a no-go criterion because we didn't have redundancy in this particular skill set. Not ideal, but now we've at least identified a gap in our capabilities and can put together a training plan to fill this gap for future operations. All of this was based on Contingency planning for walking out to the helicopter.

This level of Contingency planning, as I explained, comes with experience. Is it necessary for you to consider that somebody may choke on a banana and die at lunchtime? Of course not. For now, account for Contingencies and learn. Like anything else, practice will give you clarity.

Now for the business example. I worked with a union that had to battle regularly with a very big, high-profile, powerful corporate entity. As we were working through the Planning Process, I asked the union leaders why they thought their major initiatives were stalling. Their answer was simple: on the major initiatives, the powerful corporate entity would simply ignore union leadership's requests or put them off until the union stopped asking.

So, as we were identifying Actions for a particular plan we were working on, I asked about Contingencies. A couple were identified, but the obvious Contingency was eluding the union leaders. I reminded them that they just shared with me that their biggest obstacle to securing major initiatives for their union membership was that Corporate ignored them. I asked if it was likely that the same thing would happen for the initiative we were currently working on. Their answer was a definitive "Yes!" Yes, Corporate was definitely going to do what it always did and ignore them.

So, my question was simple: "What will you do when they ignore you?"

The first thing we had to do was give Corporate a time frame within which the leaders expected either a response or a meeting set to discuss the matter. Then, we went into

Contingency planning based on their past experience. If management ignored them again, two days past the requested time, a second email would be sent, reiterating the request and giving a new deadline. If this deadline passed, a third email would be written doing the same. If that email was ignored, an email from the union's lawyer would be sent to reiterate the request, give a new deadline, and express concern about the lack of response from management. If the lawyer was ignored, he or she would send a second email outlining possible contractual violations to the collective bargaining agreement and possible legal recourse if the union was continuously ignored. If the union still failed to get a response, they would utilize their social media accounts and publicly highlight how they were being treated before a legal grievance was filed.

Because the union leadership had unintentionally trained Corporate to ignore them without consequence, we decided on a very patient and methodical approach to Contingencies. We anticipated that Corporate would call the union's bluff at every turn, so we had to make sure that the union was willing to go the route of the most serious Contingencies of social media shaming and legal action. My very strong recommendation was not to bluff. If it meant that much to them, they should be willing to cause some discomfort and fight. If they weren't willing to go through the discomfort of social media and legal action, they should not bother making the request at all. After much discussion, they agreed it was important for many reasons and decided to execute their plan. I advised them to strap in for a bumpy ride, but I also predicted they would prevail if they followed their Contingency planning.

Sadly and predictably, Contingency after Contingency was executed. The time came for the social media campaign and legal recourse outlined by the union lawyer. The union leaders discussed abandoning the final Contingencies. After some very intense reflection, they decided to continue with their most severe Contingencies.

In a matter of hours after the social media post went out and Corporate received the planned legal action from the union's lawyer, Corporate reached out to the union leadership—not to capitulate, though. Corporate began to shame the union for acting so rashly. "Why in the world did you act so childishly by posting on social media and threatening legal action?" they asked. We anticipated this response and were ready.

The union leadership unemotionally and methodically (two behavioral guidelines they adopted) outlined the very reasonable and professional steps they took to simply get a response from Corporate. The union very simply asked at that point if Corporate was ready to talk. Amazingly, they said no, they were not. They would not be bullied, they said. The legal grievance was filed as soon as the the union hung up the phone and included the efforts they went through before they finally decided to file the grievance, i.e., their Contingency planning.

With that, Corporate was ready to talk. Much more of the same Contingency planning took place, and it was painful at times, but the union leadership prevailed. It was a great moment for them and their membership.

For years, the union had been dismissing the one Contingency that was stopping them from providing big-ticket items to their membership. When they realized there were a series of steps they could take to put pressure on Corporate after they'd been ignored, and then had the courage to take those steps, they began securing the initiatives that had previously stalled. Since then, Contingency planning has become the lifeblood of the union's ability to deliver for their membership.

Because of their ability to use Contingency planning, the relationship between the union and Corporate moved from adversarial and transactional to collaborative and partnership-based. All because they started asking the simple question, "What will we do if ... ?"

SMACCC: "Communication"

The final element of SMACCC is Communication. As I've said, if you miss an element of this Planning Process, you increase your likelihood of failure exponentially, so all elements are important.

However, Communication holds a sort of plus-one status. Why? Because if we have a good Communications plan, we'll be able to quickly identify if we missed or shortchanged any of the other elements of the Planning Process.

However, if we miss or shortchange the Communications plan, then we've just inhibited our ability to quickly identify other lapses in our plan and make the necessary small adjustments in a timely fashion, rather than massive adjustments at the last second. And making massive adjustments at the last second is what happens (only if you're lucky) when you have a poor Communications plan.

Let me break it down. If you are executing your Communications plan and ask for a status on a specific Action, and you receive no response, your first question will be one of Command. "Who is in charge of that Action?" Well, you might come to realize that Command was not assigned to that Action. Fine, now you can quickly assign Command and keep rolling. However, if you didn't have a good, consistent Communications plan you wouldn't know that Action wasn't being executed until it was too late.

As the leader, you are accountable for the overall Mission. Therefore, it is incumbent upon you to know the status of the plan. To do this, you must communicate in a consistent, methodical, and precise manner.

Decide who you will talk to, when you will talk with them, how you will talk with them (i.e., by phone, in person, video conference), for how long you will talk with them, and about what you will talk with them.

The Communications plan does not refer to the soft skills of Communication like tone of voice, delivery, body language, etc. The soft skills of Communication are extremely important, but not what we are discussing.

When you are putting together your Communications plan, consider how much of what is discussed is applicable to how many people are on the call. Will the information being presented on the call at any given time only be applicable to a small percentage of people on the call? If so, that is a lot of wasted time for the majority of the people. That's why we can't be lazy with our Communications plan and simply have an all-hands meeting once per week.

Your rule of thumb for devising your Communications plan should be that 100% of the information discussed on the call or meeting should be applicable to 100% of the people on the call or at the meeting.

All-hands calls have their place, especially at the beginning of a Mission. It's good to let everyone know what the overall Situation and Mission are, as well as a 30,000-foot view of the overall plan. But to be as efficient as possible, after that, the leader should consider more targeted calls that are shorter and specific to the audience, rather than those big, unwieldy calls where people ultimately lose focus.

The next thing to consider in your Communications plan is Communication up, down, and across the chain of Command. In other words, are you sharing the progress with your boss? Are you appropriately sharing the status of the plan with those under your charge? Are you sharing updates with those other business units that can be affected by your plan? In other words, if the success or failure of your plan can affect another business unit either positively or negatively, they need to be part of your Communications plan. This is very simply how we break down the "silos" that plague so many organizations.

Those are the six elements of SMACCC. As you can guess, there are many ways to implement SMACCC—hence, the Art of the Planning Process. We will do a deeper dive into the

Art of the Planning Process and how it is used as a leadership tool in the next chapter.

So how should we begin implementing SMACCC? I recommend you start this process by simply accounting for the elements in your plan privately. Look at what you are doing, or what you want to do, and see if you have appropriately accounted for each element of SMACCC. If you have, good! Carry on! If you have not, then account for it and carry on.

You can't go wrong by being very strict about the process, listing each element, and then filling in the blanks. This can be a little bumpy early on until you really get the hang of it, but so is anything new that is worth doing. Either way, the key is to account for the elements. Have you identified the Situation? Have you identified the clear Mission? You'll figure out your Art of applying this Planning Process as you go and will adapt to what works best for you. Eventually, your people will be in tune with the elements of the Planning Process (whether you account for the elements strictly or not), and it will become part of the language they speak as they are making, executing, adjusting, and debriefing the plan.

I've heard, "Errol, we have a planning process. We iterate," or, "We scrum."

My response to that is, "Fantastic." But you still need to know your Mission when you scrum. You still need to identify Actions and who is in Command of which Action when you iterate. The elements of SMACCC fit into, and are essential elements of, whatever you call your Planning Process, including iterating and scrumming. The same is true of project management software. The software is not your plan or your Planning Process; it is only where you house your plan. As long as you are housing the element of SMACCC somewhere in your project management software, your plan will succeed.

Thoughts and Considerations on This "Simple" Planning Process

Remember, process is not a dirty word. The creative types out there will initially feel stifled or confined when they read through the elements of SMACCC—not because SMACCC is stifling or confining but because, in their minds, they are not separating a creative idea from the *execution* of a creative idea. Those are two different conversations.

The Navy SEALs practically invented the idea of the craziest goal—jumping out of an airplane in the middle of the night, into the middle of the ocean, with all their gear, and traveling miles in the water to sneak up on and dominate an enemy that doesn't know they're coming. Does that sound like restrictive thinking? Of course not, because it isn't. We were always thinking of new and dynamic ways to do our job better.

However, when an out-of-the-box, crazy idea is put on the table, the next thing that happens is NOT, "Woohoo, let's go jump out of the airplane at night into the middle of the ocean right now! Let's go! Yeah!" Behind every unique and creative idea lies a disciplined and methodical Planning Process to make it come alive.

In fact, this process allows for even more creativity. Having a plan to execute a big idea is a natural stress limiter. As we've learned, when our brain is not under stress or in fight-or-flight mode, we are open to new suggestions or new ideas. Having a plan allows us to see from a wider lens and make necessary adjustments along the way to improve on our big idea.

For those of you who look at SMACCC and feel excited because it lays out a nice, neat place for everything and everybody, I've got some bad news for you. This won't be neat and tidy. It will be messy. Yes, the process is simple, and you probably read this and thought, "Why wasn't I doing this before? I never do this, ugh! This makes so much sense!" Don't get sucked into thinking the execution of the process will be as simple as the process appears. It won't be. But that's OK because neat and tidy isn't the goal. Mission accomplishment is the goal.

When we have a process, we are able to look back and see where things went right and where things went wrong. When we can look back with this kind of clarity, we can determine what things need to stay and what things need improvement or need to go. You may reflect on the elements of SMACCC and determine that you intuitively do most of the things already. That's fine, but operating on intuition isn't good enough. Intuition does not allow you to go back through what happened in a clear, concise, methodical fashion to unemotionally evaluate where and why things went right or wrong. Only adhering to a process does that. If you can't seem to break through with the big idea, it's likely because you are acting on intuition alone. The Planning Process will allow you to see for yourself which of your intuitions can be trusted and which ones cannot.

As a leader, you are expected to guide, train, and teach your people whenever possible, and intuition cannot be taught, guided, or trained. You cannot hold people accountable for your intuition. Expectations based on intuition are not clear and do not provide for a safe, predictable environment.

Do you know what a leader can teach, guide, and make clear what people will be held accountable for? The elements of SMACCC.

One final note: These are the elements of a Planning Process that are used to keep people alive and achieve Mission accomplishment on the battlefield. This process was not formulated by academics in a sterile lab. It is literally born of blood. Keep an open mind when you start employing SMACCC. Account for the elements in everything you do, even if they are not applicable, which sometimes they won't be. Be patient with yourself, and you'll get the hang of it with practice.

The Planning Process as a Leadership Tool

Now THAT WE'VE GONE THROUGH THE ELEMENTS OF SMACCC and how to use them to make a plan that will succeed, let's discuss how the Planning Process, in conjunction with some behavioral guidelines, can be used as a leadership tool. The examples I'm going to provide are by no means the only examples of how SMACCC can be used as a leadership tool, but they are some of the most common I've come across and allow you to take the Art of the Planning Process, and your leadership effectiveness, to a whole new level.

Instilling Initiative and Autonomy: Hear the Plan First

Let's start with how SMACCC allows us to instill initiative and autonomy in our people while also giving us the ability to have a full situational awareness of the overall workflow. It's the leader's job to understand the overall Situation and set the Mission, as we discussed in the last chapter.

But once we have identified and communicated the Situation and Mission, we hand over the responsibility of how that Mission will be accomplished to our people. In other words, you tell your people the Mission, and they tell you how they are going to accomplish that Mission through Actions, Command, Contingencies, and Communication. It is as simple as that. Tell them what you want them to achieve and why you want them to achieve it, and then let them get to work to figure out how they are going to do it by focusing on the elements of SMACCC.

Empowering your people in this way to act with initiative and autonomy does not mean you have no idea what your people are doing or what decisions they are making. So, when you give them the Mission and ask them to tell you how they are going to accomplish that Mission, you must hear their plan before they begin executing. That is your job as a leader: to know what your people's plan is before they begin executing. When you hear the plan before execution begins, everyone is clear under what parameters they have full authority to make decisions or to act autonomously.

What If I Don't Like Their Plan?

The challenge for you as a leader is to understand and accept that your people may tackle an objective differently than you. This can be hard initially, but it is an absolute requirement for proper delegation. What happens if you, the leader, are listening to the plan and are not comfortable with it?

Maybe you are not comfortable with the plan because it's not how you would do it, so you need more convincing that it will work. Maybe it consists of elements that, based on your experience, you are confident will not work because they have been tried before and met with failure. How do we challenge the elements of a plan as a leader while not stripping away the initiative and autonomy we are trying to create in our people?

Well, the obvious answer is that you need to ask questions. But you need to ask the right kind of questions. The most common way leaders ask questions to challenge a plan is, "Have you considered doing it this way or that way?" You may even add that it's up to them which way they decide, that you're just making a recommendation—providing food for thought. You may even really mean it. Or, maybe you're hoping they'll just take the hint and do it your way. Either way, there is a serious problem with asking a question or making a suggestion in this way.

The problem is that leaders don't make suggestions. They give orders. When you make a suggestion, your employee will likely think to themselves, "Well, if I don't take the boss's suggestion, and my way doesn't work, that will look bad for me, and I'll have to contend with some form of, 'I told you so.'" To be safe, your employee will just do it your way. They may still feel strongly about doing it their way but don't want to deal with any potential resentment or hard feelings if they come to you and say, "Thanks for your recommendation, but I'm not going to take it. I'm going to go ahead and do it my way." For the employee to deliver a message like this to the boss is easier said than done, and they shouldn't be put in that position in the first place.

This simple breakdown makes it clear that this way of asking a question or giving a suggestion does not create or instill initiative or autonomy. It's just another form of giving an order, whether you mean it to be or not. When this happens, it's no longer their plan. Now, it's your plan that they are simply executing. They are not thinking or using their initiative. They are just executing your checklist. This doesn't create thinkers and doers who have skin in the game. It creates robots.

Challenging the Plan and Still Letting It Be Theirs

You should be able to challenge the plan. That's your job. But how do you do it in a way that keeps the plan theirs but still challenges their thought process? Once again, SMACCC has the answer. You ask your questions, or make your challenges, in the form of Contingencies.

Let's say you are being briefed on a series of Actions, and you are not comfortable with them. You see some holes. So, you simply ask, "What will you do if this thing happens?" You obviously have something in mind based on your experience, so just ask what they will do if that particular thing happens that will disrupt the Action.

One of two things will happen. First, they'll have an answer. Good! That means they are thinking and have a clear direction if that Contingency arises. It still may not be how you would do it, but now they've shown you they have thought through potential problems and have earned the opportunity to execute their way because their plan has stood up to scrutiny. And, in the process, maybe you've learned something.

The second thing that can happen is they won't have an answer. Suppose you pose the question, "What will you do if this thing happens?" and they answer with, "I don't know." Well, now you get to make recommendations or suggestions and then ask them to come back with an updated plan. You've done your job. You've appropriately imparted some of your wisdom and experience because it was solicited. You asked a question, and they did not have an answer, so you provided some suggestions to kick-start their thought process.

By challenging their plan in the form of Contingency questions, you have begun to train your people to think beyond simple Actions by being aware of Contingencies. You've also allowed them to keep the plan their own by asking them to come back with an updated version. It's still their plan!

You've created thinkers because now they know you will challenge their plans through Contingency questioning. Now they will begin to think in Contingencies to challenge their own plan before they present it to you because you have made it a clear expectation, or Guideline for Behavior, that they can expect from you. That's how you develop thinkers, encourage initiative and autonomy, and make it clear what your people will be held accountable for.

I'm Afraid I'll Lose Track of What's Happening, but I Don't Want to Micromanage

How do you keep track of what's happening without micromanaging? First, let's define micromanaging. Micromanaging is giving a checklist of things to do or telling people how to do what you want them to do.

Receiving updates on what they said they were going to do is not micromanaging. Call it "microknowledging," or call it whatever you want. But minimally, call it your job. It is your job to know what your people are doing and the status of the plan. How do we do this? The Communications portion of SMACCC.

When we make a Communications plan, we set the parameters for our Communication. We establish the day, time, place, topic, and length of the meeting. The first thing you've done when the parameters for your Communications plan have been set is establish what someone will be held accountable for: an update on this topic (or Action) on this date and time.

Next, you will be able to focus your conversation because you already know what you will be updated about based on the plan. "I will update you on this Action on this day and time." Now we are not wasting time. The meeting is focused, and 100% of the information being discussed is applicable to 100% of the people in the conversation.

You have now received a specific update on the plan you are overseeing. Does this sound like micromanaging? Of course, it doesn't because it's not. Having a good, consistent

Communications plan allows you to stay up-to-date about what is happening without micromanaging your people.

A word of warning: If someone resists providing regular, targeted updates, or complains that you are micromanaging because you are asking for an update, you likely have a problem on your hands. As we have discussed, getting updates is not micromanaging. Additionally, who doesn't want to provide the boss with a good update? Someone who doesn't have something good to update, that's who. You may have to dive a little deeper into what this person is doing.

More Bad Questions

You've done the work as a leader. You've provided the Situation and Mission and asked for a plan to accomplish the Mission BEFORE work started. You've given your people the initiative and autonomy they crave by properly delegating the nuts and bolts of the plan to those who will be doing the work.

You've challenged their plans through Contingency questions. You have forced your people to think a couple of steps ahead in the plan, and you've also taught them to do this on their own because they know you will be asking them, "What will you do if?" questions. You've developed thinkers and doers!

You are not losing track of the status of the plan because a good, consistent Communications plan was made. You are getting regular, targeted updates. You are not wasting your people's time because 100% of the information on your calls is applicable to 100% of the people on the call.

And after all this great leadership work, you do this: "Let me know if you need anything!"

Or you might ask, "What can I do to help?"

Your intentions are good, but this stands out like a sore thumb compared to all the good leadership work done up until this point. The purpose of all the work up to this point is so you, the leader, can actually identify specifically where you can help by asking questions about the topic of the scheduled Communication. What do I mean?

If there is an Action, we know from the last chapter that that Action should have a date by which it will be completed. One of the obvious areas of discussion during your update is whether or not that Action will be completed on schedule. If it is clear the answer is yes, then your employee probably doesn't need any help with anything right now. Good! Tell them, "Great work!" and let them be on their way.

If the answer is, "No, we're going to be late," the obvious question for the leader to ask is "Why?" Ask, "Why?" and then listen.

For example, you ask, "Why?" and your employee tells you that the Action will not be completed on time because it is simply taking longer than expected. That's fine. It happens.

Then perhaps they go on to tell you that everyone is working overtime, and the Action will only be a week late. "We'll get it done. Don't worry."

As a leader, you should be proud of that reaction. It's "can do." It's ownership. It's all good. But maybe your employee is so focused on getting the job done that they are not clearly identifying areas where they need help. But you, the leader, can identify those areas.

This is where the Communications plan has become a leadership tool by identifying where your people need help. "The task is just taking longer than we expected, but we'll work overtime to get it done." As the leader, I love the spirit, but as we discussed in Cultural Awareness and Recognition, that is not a sustainable solution. Is "working overtime to get it done" a sustainable and transferable behavior that you want to make up your culture? It's only important to go the "extra mile" and "buckle down" and show "grit" when it's important to show those things, which should only be sparingly. If that is how you are constantly doing business, then there is a problem.

Are you helping your employee if your response to them is, "OK, just tell me what you need,"? I don't think so. There are a couple of other obvious, more targeted, questions you could ask that would likely drill down on a more specific cause of the delay in question. "Do you need more resources? Will another person help?" "Are you getting the support from the other business units that was promised?" "Are there gaps in skill set or training that are slowing you down?"

The point is that a good, consistent Communications plan should allow the leader to ask targeted questions about the status of the Mission, identify problems before they become too big, and provide the necessary assistance or solution when the employee may not see it. If your go-to as a leader is, "Just let me know what you need," then you are either not listening to the updates, or they are not being held consistently enough for you to have a firm grasp on the big picture.

It's Their Plan, Shouldn't They See the Problems?

As we continue with our example, it begs the question, "Why won't they see the cause for delay? It's their plan. Shouldn't they know why it is stalling?" They may not see it, or claim not to see it, for a lot of reasons. Maybe they are ashamed or hesitant to ask for help because you might think they are not capable if they ask for more resources. Maybe they don't have enough experience to even know what to ask for. Maybe they have lost the forest through the trees and cannot see the obvious. That is why asking, "Is there anything you need?" or stating something grand but ultimately meaningless is not what leaders should be doing. Your people may not know what they need.

Get a clear and concise update based on the Communication portion of the plan, and you'll see what the challenges are or where your people need assistance. That's what leaders do. They see the problems before they become unmanageable and help make the small adjustments early. This is to say nothing of the fact that you are giving your people the personal and targeted attention that builds real human connection. Leaders do this by focusing on the Communications plan and using SMACCC as a leadership tool.

SMACCC and Finding Calm Amidst the Chaos

Let's now move to how SMACCC can limit anxiety and allow you to perform in a calm and clear manner under stress. More often than not, stress and anxiety are caused by uncertainty or the feeling that things are out of control—or, more specifically, out of *our* control.

We very often experience this stress and anxiety because we simply don't know how things are going to turn out. There is enough uncertainty to go around, so we should take every opportunity to create certainty where we can. How do we do that? By having a plan.

If we follow the elements of SMACCC, when chaos ensues we can go back to our Mission and ask ourselves, "OK, things seem a little out of control. What are we actually trying to achieve?" When we do that ... when we remind ourselves what our Mission is, we can evaluate what Actions people are taking and determine if they drive Mission accomplishment. If they don't, you as the leader can begin refocusing people's Actions. If they do, then there is nothing to worry about because people are acting toward Mission accomplishment. We've created certainty by knowing what people should be doing based on the clearly identified Mission. Common sense, but not always common practice.

A good example of limiting anxiety through the use of SMACCC is deadline management. Deadlines should never sneak up on a leader because the leader should already know the status of everyone's work. How? Because the leader has implemented and followed an effective Communications plan. With an effective Communications plan, the leader is getting regular, concise updates from their people. A week out from any deadline, a leader should already know if the project will meet, be ahead, or be behind the deadline date. When you already know the outcome of something and can communicate *why* to the applicable parties ahead of time (like your own boss), there is nothing to be anxious about.

Even in the "worst case" scenario of being late to the deadline, if you communicate and are aware ahead of time you will be behind schedule, then that means you've also done the work of understanding why you are behind schedule. You can make the necessary adjustments and communicate this "bad news" unemotionally, methodically, and with confidence.

But It's Not Always That Cut and Dry

Having a plan ahead of time creates certainty, and certainty in and of itself is a stress limiter. But what about those times when a real emergency arises? When something serious and truly unexpected thrusts itself upon you and your team? How do you handle these Situations with the calm and confidence of a leader? It may not be something you planned for, but that's OK because you know HOW to make a plan.

In moments of stress, we default to what we know. We go to the behaviors that have been ingrained in our brains and are habits. So, this begs the question: What do you know? Some people know panic. Some people know blame. Some people know retreat. Some people know excuses. What should you know? Know a Planning Process. Know SMACCC. Knowing a Planning Process allows you to take the emotion out of an otherwise emotional Situation.

In the first element of the leadership process, Emotional Awareness and Recognition, we talked about the non-leadership process of Action: TRIGGER to EMOTION directly to ACTION. Then we discussed needing to add THINK and DECIDE to change the leadership thought process to TRIGGER to EMOTION to THINK/DECIDE to ACTION. That's all well and good, as long as you know what to do inside of THINK and DECIDE. What should you do inside of THINK and DECIDE? Have a plan! Go through SMACCC.

Here is a combat example to bring this point home—the first time I was shot at in Afghanistan. Obviously, the trigger is getting shot at. I felt many emotions at that moment, which was fine. We don't limit ourselves to one emotion because we can have several competing emotions at the same time.

I felt a rush of excitement and exhilaration. I also felt surprise and the obvious rush of fear. That was no time to hope my Actions were appropriate. In that instance, I had to know what my Actions were going to be, or else I'd suffer the worst of all consequences: Mission failure, injury, or death. All unacceptable.

So, TRIGGER, getting shot at. EMOTION, excitement, fear, surprise, exhilaration. I then went immediately to THINK and DECIDE ... SMACCC. The Situation was this: I was getting shot at, and the rush of emotions and adrenaline through my body were about to make me fall down and relinquish my responsibilities in the patrol—a deadly proposition for those who were counting on me to do my job and watch their back. Did this fit the Situation fact check? Is your response to this, "Well, what did you do about that?" You bet your ass it did! I was able to define the Situation clearly. Good start!

My Mission was simple: physically get control of myself so I could carry out my duties.

My Actions were simple: Acknowledge the impact my emotions were having on what was happening. This allowed me to understand that the sudden onset of all those emotions created an adrenaline rush in my body that temporarily weakened my legs, better known as an adrenaline dump. Having that in my conscious mind allowed me to avoid dwelling on it and focus on my next Actions: Identify where the shots were coming from, identify my field of fire, locate a target, locate the other members of the patrol. In short, get back to the standard operating procedures associated with being shot at and not let external circumstances control how I responded.

My Contingencies were also simple: If I succumbed to the adrenaline dump and fell, I would simply get back up. Is that common sense? Of course, it was. But remember, we were dealing with a high-stress, life-and-death Situation that could easily cloud any rational thought. Because I was going through that process, falling would not have fazed me in the least because I was fully aware of everything that was happening and why it was happening. I did not have the added stress of the unknown, I went exactly to what I knew. And on the SMACCC process went ...

The point is, I went to what I knew in a true moment of crisis and was able to do it quickly and with clarity. Because I made a habit of Emotional Awareness and Recognition and had control of my Actions by employing SMACCC inside of THINK and DECIDE, I was able to act professionally and calmly during a true moment of stress and danger. I was able to use the SMACCC we had planned before the incident, and I was able to enact a new SMACCC in the midst of it.

Of course, moments of stress and danger will vary from the battlefield to the boardroom, to the kitchen table. But the process for remaining and acting calm under stress is the same: Know a Planning Process, make a plan, and execute that plan. Go to what you know and know a Planning Process. Know SMACCC to stay calm amidst the chaos.

SMACCC! Your Brain Is Paying Attention; Rewiring and Prioritizing

YOU'RE SITTING ON THE COUCH WATCHING *AMERICAN GANGSTER* for the umpteenth time, eating chicken wings and chips and salsa. The last time you watched it, you drank a few too many Budweisers, so today you are going to go with Bud Light or Coke. As you are enjoying the movie (again), you realize it's been a while since you did any exercise. Actually, you realize it's been a while since you read a book, went to a museum, or did anything in your free time other than watch *American Gangster* and eat crappy food.

This makes you feel a little bad. You are not proud of yourself. So, you boldly proclaim (to yourself) that you are going to change ... tomorrow! Then you throw another chicken wing to the back of your throat as you contemplate how great tomorrow will look. But you don't want to contemplate it too much because the good part of the movie is coming up.

Do you know what your brain is doing at that moment? Laughing at you. That's not the scientific term, but it might as well be. Your brain knows you are not serious because your

Actions did not even come close to your "conviction." You said something and just sat there doing the same old thing. Your brain did not create any new chemicals because no new emotion was created. No new chemicals were sent to the body from the brain because no new Action was taken to create a new experience which creates new emotions. Tomorrow will look just like today, count on it.

But, you can play out the same scenario with a twist: This time, instead of just sitting there doing the same thing (because you are going to start tomorrow), you start to make a plan. Instead of throwing the next chicken wing to the back of your throat, you put it down and focus on making a plan for how you're going to begin turning your life around.

Do you know what your brain is doing now? It's paying attention. Why is it paying attention? Because this is a new experience. As you go through the elements of the Planning Process, your brain is creating new synaptic connections and sending new chemicals to the body. You are literally changing the physiology of your mind and your body by making a plan.

You write your plan down according to the elements of SMACCC. You can now see your purpose (Situation) and focus (Mission). Because we have purpose and focus, our brain is less scattered. We know from previous chapters that when our brain is less scattered and more focused, it relaxes. When the brain relaxes, it opens your ability to see things from a broader perspective and be more creative.

When your brain is relaxed and more creative, you can practice metacognition. You are aware of what you are doing and what you are feeling.[72] Because you are practicing meta-cognition, or being in the moment, you are aware of when you are not executing the Actions in your plan, and you can quickly move back to them so you never get too far off course. You are creating a new mind because you are following your plan.

As you focus on your plan, you begin to see in your mind what you want to achieve. When you see what you want to achieve, you become happy, content, and inspired. You are now creating a new chemical reality in your body and mind based on these new emotions. And they are elevated emotions—not the old ugly emotions of hidden guilt, shame, and worthlessness you were feeling but suppressing while sitting on the couch, watching television, and eating junk food.

You run into a stumbling block as you are performing the Actions to your plan. But instead of stressing out and quitting, you readjust because you've accounted for some of the predictable stumbles you might face along the way (Contingencies). Because of this, you are quickly back on track. Your brain continues to change as it adapts to your new Actions. It starts to strengthen those synaptic connections in your brain based on your new behaviors, thoughts, and emotions.

You are following your plan, making necessary adjustments along the way, and you are making progress. You begin to focus on how you are feeling now and how you will feel in the future. These, once again, are elevated emotions. The ones that

---

72   Dispenza, Dr. Joe. *Breaking the Habit of Being Yourself: How to Lose Your Mind and Create a New One*. 1st ed. Carlsbad, CA: Hay House, 2012.

up-regulate our genes and make us healthy. And now you have begun to flip the script on those past, negative emotions and thoughts that you've repeated over and over again. The ones that science tells us down-regulate our genes and make us sick.[73]

Now instead of dwelling on a negative emotion of the past (worthlessness and guilt for your past behaviors?) and allowing those negative emotions to dominate your present and future thinking (like we know they will), you are allowing the positive emotions of the future to dominate your present and future thinking. Now your behavioral change takes another sharp turn for the positive because your brain and body are now becoming neurochemically addicted to THESE behaviors and thoughts.

When we make a plan, we are signaling to our brain that we are serious, and it reacts in kind as I just described. These are broad strokes of science, but they are accurate and show the power of planning from a scientific view, in case you hadn't already bought in.

Practicing the Art with Cold Exposure

As you've noticed, we can practice the Art of each element of the leadership process with cold exposure. The difference is the intention we put behind each practice session in the cold. Again, another Guideline for Behavior to practice with

---

73   Dispenza, Dr. Joe. *Becoming Supernatural: How Common People Are Doing the Uncommon.* 2nd ed. Carlsbad, CA: Hay House, 2019.

cold exposure is Acting with intention. If you did everything with clear intention, would you get better? Of course, you would! That makes Acting with intention a good Guideline for Behavior to consider.

So, what is our intention in stepping into the cold as it relates to SMACCC? Cold exposure is a tool to help you consider the elements of SMACCC as a matter of course and habit in your day-to-day life. This is so important because as you get good at this, you will realize that the need for considering the elements of SMACCC are everywhere in our lives.

Let's look at how applying SMACCC to an ice bath might work to help you get into the rhythm of SMACCC:

Situation. (Set of circumstances dictating the need for Action):
     The Planning Process is new to me, and I want to be able to
     seamlessly integrate it into my leadership skills.

Mission. (Your goal or what you want to accomplish): To
     consciously cover each one of the elements of SMACCC
     before, during, and after the ice bath.

Actions (The things you will do to accomplish your Mission):

   1. Identify my emotions before I enter the ice bath.
   2. Exercise THINK/DECIDE as part of the TRIGGER to
      EMOTION to THINK/DECIDE to ACT.
   3. Determine how I want to behave (Guidelines for
      Behavior) when I consider THINK/DECIDE, i.e, I

want to act professionally and not show excessive and unnecessary emotional responses. I want to show courage and move to get into the ice bath quickly without procrastination.

4. Enter the ice bath in a calm, methodical fashion.

5. Recognize the fight-or-flight response (sympathetic nervous system) as I get in the water (breath being taken away), and remember this is a normal response.

6. Find my breath through a purposeful exhale which will serve to calm me down by activating the vagus nerve. Continue to focus only on my breath by breathing in through my nose and exhaling either through my nose or mouth, eventually getting to a long, gentle nasal breathing pattern.

7. Focus my attention on my breath. When my mind wanders to external thoughts like how cold the water is, how much longer I should stay in, or how much I hate this, bring my mind back to my breath.

8. Once I find and maintain my breath through a long, gentle breathing pattern, exit the ice bath in a calm, methodical manner.

9. Once out, take the horse stance position (deep bend at the knees, wide stance) and move my upper body and arms from side to side to begin to warm myself in space. Maintain a strict focus on this movement, and when my mind wanders to an external thought (I need to get a towel and sweatshirt!), bring my mind back to my breath and movement.

Contingencies. (Consider things that can go wrong as I execute Actions and account for them):

1. I feel the need to immediately exit the water or make some overly dramatic gesture like yelling, "Oh, shit, this is cold!": I will remind myself that this type of reaction is normal and refocus on finding my breath and behaving in a professional and courageous manner.

2. I struggle to calm my breathing down: I will continue to act with professionalism and courage and not succumb to the urge to exit the ice. I will exaggerate my exhale to force the activation of my vagus nerve to calm myself down. When my mind wanders from my breath, I will bring focus back to it. If necessary, I will exit the ice bath, refocus on my plan, and try it again.

3. The pain in my fingers and toes becomes unbearable, even though I have found my breath and am otherwise remaining calm amidst the chaos of the ice bath: I will understand that this is nothing more than an environmental response to the cold called vasoconstriction. Since I am new to ice baths and have successfully found my breath and calm, I will simply end the ice bath because there is no reason to endure unnecessary pain. As I grow more experienced, I know my body will eventually adapt, and the pain will subside, and I will begin to endure small amounts of discomfort a little at a time until I have found the ability to seamlessly adapt to this response with little to no discomfort.

Command. I and I alone am in Command of my Actions. Outside influences or thoughts have nothing to do with my ability to execute on my Actions to achieve my Mission.

Communication. I will check in with my breathing and focus continuously by practicing metacognition. I will check in with myself constantly to ensure I am aware of what I am doing and aware of what I am feeling. (Or, this section could be "not applicable." It doesn't matter, as long as you have accounted for it.)

If you make this plan BEFORE you get into the ice bath, your chances of achieving all the things you want to achieve are undeniably excellent!

Bringing It into the Office

To begin getting the hang of the Planning Process consider past, present, and future initiatives.

Past: Recall an initiative that met with substandard results, straight failure, or stagnation. Now go through the elements of SMACCC, and see if one was not accounted for and how this affected the overall progress of the initiative. Get ready for some scary revelations.

Present: Every day, identify at least one of the elements of SMACCC you are executing on a current project. Perhaps you redefined or clarified an overall Mission. Perhaps you are executing part of your Communications plan by getting an update from a subordinate or are updating another business unit yourself. The point of this is simple: if you can't identify that the Actions you are taking throughout the day are contributing to Mission success, then you'll need to re-evaluate what you and your team are actually doing. This may end up being a painful drill, but it will make clear very quickly how targeted your and your team's workflow is.

Future: Think ahead to initiatives that are being considered or are on the board for future execution. Go through each element of SMACCC and consider how thoroughly each has been considered, especially Situation and Mission. Consider resources available for Command to undertake the Actions necessary for Mission accomplishment. Consider the Situation. Do you know why the initiative is being undertaken? If you know why, does it merit Action now, or can it wait?

This is an excellent way to become accustomed to SMACCC. You'll be less emotionally attached to a past objective that may not have gone as you would have liked, and you'll be able to clearly assess what elements of SMACCC you may have missed or short-changed. This will give you great awareness of what is currently happening in a project, so you can make your necessary adjustments. Finally, you'll be in a great position to have a full plan in place for your future project, and you'll start to see the benefits of planning before you act.

SMACCC and Prioritization

Let's now address prioritization and how SMACCC, combined with proper behavioral guidelines, can help with this leadership challenge. Everybody is busy, there's a lot to do and not enough time to do it. What happens so often is we end up with what seems like 100 things going on at once. So, we write a to-do list and try to knock out a little on each task every day.

This makes us feel good. We are working hard on all our responsibilities. But, if you look at it closer, it's a losing proposition. Why? Because responsibilities keep getting added. So, if you are working on them all a little at a time, how can we expect to get any of them fully completed?

The more this pattern happens, the more it seems like all you are doing is putting out fires because you are continuously adding things to your to-do list without actually knocking any of them off. That feeling of putting out fires all day every day comes down to prioritization.

Let's say, based on the challenge of properly prioritizing, we adopt a behavior guideline that's part of Navy SEAL combat ethos to prioritize and execute. (I like to add Prioritize and Execute to Completion). Remember, If we didn't change the way we made, marketed, or sold our widget but behaved in these ways, would we get better? If we prioritized and executed to completion, would this make us better? Of course, so that makes it a good behavioral guideline. But, HOW do we prioritize?

This is where SMACCC helps us. First, identify the Situation for each project or task you are working on or need to work on. The Situation is the set of circumstances dictating a need for Action.

Let's say your SEAL patrol gets ambushed, and one or more of your teammates has been shot and needs assistance. You've got two Situations at play here. First, you've been ambushed. The enemy has located you, got the drop on you, and is shooting at you. Second, you have operators down and injured. Without the proper medical assistance, they will die.

Combat is the ultimate expression of consequence. And in this instance, if the leader doesn't correctly prioritize which Situation they will act on first, the ultimate consequences will be realized: Mission failure, more injury, or death. All unacceptable.

Both Situations are dire, and both need to be addressed as soon as possible. The first challenge is to realize you have two Situations at play that will require separate Missions. We need to fight back, and we need to save our teammates' lives. But if we try to do them both at the same time, we will lose the fight, lose the lives of those who are already injured, and likely get more people killed. That lesson has been learned in blood—hence the combat ethos—or behavior, to prioritize and execute to completion.

Given the two Situations and their corresponding Missions, we must now unemotionally and methodically decide which one needs to be prioritized. Unemotional and methodical, by the way, is another behavior that makes us better, especially in this example.

We love our teammates and every instinct in our fiber tells us to go to them immediately and save their lives. However, the incoming fire from our adversary is the priority. Because if we don't suppress the fire from the enemy, we will continue to take casualties and lose lives. So, as distasteful as it seems, we must prioritize and first engage the enemy and suppress their fire before we move to help our teammates.

In this example, the behavior of prioritize and execute sets us on the right path. We follow SMACCC, identify the importance of the Situations and Missions in play, and use an unemotional and methodical behavior to properly prioritize and begin executing. How do we execute? Continue to follow the elements of SMACCC—it's nothing more than a plan we need to execute. And the elements of SMACCC allow us to execute any plan at any time.

The key here is that we could not have possibly prioritized if we did not identify and separate the multiple Situations and Missions in play. While combat highlights the importance of following the leadership process, let's once again bring it back to the boardroom.

In our combat example, we are forced to prioritize suppressing the enemy fire over coming to the aid of our teammates while we listen to their pleas of, "Help me! Help me!" If we can prioritize over those human pleas, which we can, we can surely handle the indignation someone at the office may feel when we ask them "Why?" or "What's the Situation?" in order to properly assess and effectively prioritize their request for something to be done immediately.

Our injured teammates in my combat example know we must suppress enemy fire first. They know we must prioritize and execute before we move on to the next task of saving their lives. It doesn't mean they don't still beg you to make an exception. But, they know HOW WE DO BUSINESS! They know the established Guidelines for Behavior. They know their teammates are acting with Emotional Awareness and Recognition, so they can act in the overall best interest of the group. They know we are following the elements of SMACCC, so we will get to them as fast as possible.

If following the elements of SMACCC is good enough to save lives and find victory on the battlefield, it's good enough to consider for your team. Make identifying the Situation and properly prioritizing based on the Situation and Mission the way your team does business, and you will be relieved of the daily fires we use as an excuse to underperform from day to day.

The Challenge of Technology and Prioritization

If you are in the world of technology, this scenario should sound familiar to you. I have come across it countless times working with technology companies and technology engineers.

You are the leader of a software engineering team. You have just been advised that there is a new customer ready to sign a large contract and several existing customers ready to not only renew but also expand their current contracts.

Typically, there are several new features the clients want to be built into the platform before the deals are finalized. You are getting pressure from every angle to incorporate the new features immediately so the deals can be closed and the company can realize its end-of-the-year revenue goals. Without the deals, the company will fall short of its year-end projections. However, your platform has become unstable and will not likely be able to support the new features for an acceptable amount of time.

Again, you have a few Situations at play here. New business and current contracts are being renewed and expanded as long as new features are added to the platform. Meeting year-end earnings goals is contingent upon these deals being closed immediately. Your platform is currently unstable, and you are not sure how well it can support the new, required features.

You get the point. Here we can identify three separate Situations at play and decide which one needs to be handled first. This is a sticky scenario, but a common one. As you prioritize based on the competing Situations, you can clearly identify your Missions and the remaining portions of the plan. You will very likely need to stabilize your platform first and foremost (at least, that has been the most successful path I've seen taken in these scenarios). If that is your top priority, then the Communication aspect of your plan, as is usually the case, becomes all the more important. You've got to explain that the features your customers desire can't be added until the platform is stabilized.

This isn't the best news, but when it's communicated in an honest, logical, organized, and unemotional fashion to the client, the chances are you've just increased your trust level with them. And you've done this because you prioritized based on competing, but clearly identified, Situations. This is how a leader uses SMACCC to prioritize and make the best decisions for their clients, team, and organization.

Big Picture Prioritization and Biting Off More Than You Can Chew

SMACCC makes clear what the required elements of a good plan are. So, when we make a plan, we are identifying the resources we will use and the timeline we will be following. As you've seen, a good plan takes a lot of work. It can use a lot of resources and take more time than we anticipated.

When we are asked to tackle another task and begin that Planning Process immediately, we must run it up against the plan that is already in motion. Do we have the time and the resources to undergo two tasks simultaneously? If you do, go for it. If you don't, you have a decision to make. You now must prioritize which project you will focus on based on the knowledge that you can't effectively focus on two at the same time because of limited resources, time, budget, or all three.

The number of projects running simultaneously can be four or five depending on the size of your organization, but the point remains the same. SMACCC shows you the resources and time it will take to complete a Mission, and this will make it clear that prioritization is not only important, but it's also a requirement of ongoing Mission accomplishment. Mission accomplishment is what is expected of leaders.

Let the plans show how many things can be done at once. Then, prioritization simply becomes a matter of course if you are paying attention to SMACCC.

Meeting Focus and Disputes

Meetings are a challenge for even the best-run organizations. Maybe you are having too many meetings. Perhaps the meetings last too long. Is 100% of the content being presented in the meeting applicable to 100% of the people in the meeting? Can you walk out of your meetings and clearly articulate why the meeting was being held, what the goal of the meeting was, and if it was accomplished? Did the meeting stay on point or move from topic to topic like shifting winds?

Having an agenda for a meeting is an excellent place to start, but it's not enough because discussion on a particular agenda item can still be unwieldy or unfocused. As the leader, it is your job to ensure that projects move toward Mission accomplishment. Therefore, the topics covered during a meeting and the questions you ask during a meeting are critical.

Remember, you can't hold people accountable if they don't know what they are supposed to be accountable for. When people know what they are supposed to be accountable for, it creates a predictable environment. There is enough unpredictability to go around. Let's create the predictability where we can because when we do that, we'll be better equipped to handle the unpredictability that will inevitably find us.

So, what should we hold people accountable for during meetings? Why not the elements of SMACCC? If these are the elements that make a successful plan, why wouldn't they be the elements people are required to address during a meeting? If people knew they were going to be accountable for the elements of SMACCC during the meeting, and they addressed those elements, would the meeting run more efficiently with the most important elements of the plan covered? Would you cover more in less time? Yes, you would.

I presented this concept to a leadership team who was struggling with their meetings. One of my first orders of business with this client was to sit in on their weekly meetings. They were usually scheduled for an hour but always went at least twice as long. Furthermore, what had actually been accomplished during the meeting was difficult to discern.

As a fix (in addition to an actual meeting agenda), we put forward that nobody could speak unless it addressed one of the elements of SMACCC. It was an initially painful process as it seemed I was doing most of the talking early on by interrupting and asking which element of SMACCC was being addressed. It was clear to everyone that the meetings were essentially free-for-alls with everyone just sounding off with random thoughts and opinions.

However, with a little guidance and discipline, it was only a few weeks until the meetings were highly productive, professional, and short—all because we kept the discussion limited to only the most essential elements that everyone knew they would be held accountable for, those of SMACCC.

What of disputes during meetings, whether the meetings are informal or formal? If you've ever really listened to a dispute, you'll find that the parties involved are often not even talking about the same thing. They are just trying to get their points or opinions across, or they're finger-pointing. Sound familiar?

How does a leader get people back on point and focused? By asking two simple questions: "Why are we here?" (Situation) and, "What are we trying to accomplish?" (Mission). When I say ask two simple questions, I mean actually ask them. And don't ask the questions rhetorically. Wait for an answer. What you will likely find is that the parties arguing don't have the same answers to those questions. And if they don't have the same answers to those very basic, operational questions, then that means they are having an argument about different things.

It's very tough to settle a dispute when the people involved are talking about different things. Get alignment and agreement on the Situation and Mission, and the disputes will move very quickly to problem-solving. When the leader gets alignment on Situation and Mission, they can bring the conversation back to a specific place when it begins to veer off course, which it will.

When someone purposely or un-purposely brings up a point, however valid, that is not in alignment with the clearly identified Situation or Mission, the leader can easily and appropriately redirect by saying something to the effect of, "Valid point. But that's a different conversation. Let's stay focused on this Situation and Mission." They may not like having their amazing point turned away, but they will know "why" and that the "why" makes sense.

Try this for meetings, whether it's a team meeting, a leadership meeting, or maybe you've joined a board of directors, and you're figuring out how to add value. Write down the elements of SMACCC, Situation, Mission, Actions, Command, Contingencies, Communication, and put them in front of you during meetings. Check off the element when it has been covered during the meeting. If you haven't heard an element covered, ask yourself if it is applicable or not. A word of caution, you may find this drill disturbing initially because so many of the elements of SMACCC won't be covered.

To add real value, when you see an element of SMACCC has not been covered, chime in with, "I'm sorry, but I wasn't clear on who was overall in charge of this initiative." Alternatively, you could say, "This sounds great, but I'm not clear on what the specific goal is. Can we clarify exactly what we are trying to accomplish?" When we keep the questions simple and focus on the important elements of a plan, SMACCC, the impact will be profound and often (silently) deafening.

So, again, leaders keep focus on Mission accomplishment and know what questions to ask. During meetings, the elements of SMACCC will keep you Mission-focused and will give you a guide as to what questions to ask to fill in gaps. It will also allow you to diffuse and appropriately redirect confrontations. This is how leaders manage meetings.

Put It to Work

Practice this concept every day! Every day, identify how you used SMACCC as a leadership tool. How did you ask questions? How did you redirect poor behavior? How did you remain calm under stressful Situations? The most common problems we face every day can be brought back to incorporating SMACCC into every aspect of our lives. Use SMACCC and change how your brain is rewired. Use SMACCC and change your neurochemical makeup. Use SMACCC and have an understanding of why things went wrong in the past so you can avoid the same mistakes in the future.

Now go make a plan and execute toward Mission accomplishment, because that's what leaders do!

Element Five—Facing the Resistance

GREAT LEADERSHIP IS ABOUT SOMETHING BIGGER THAN yourself, and it doesn't matter who, where, or what you are leading. The Ice Cold Leader Methodology is a common sense approach that is easy to understand. Follow it, and you will find success as a leader in every aspect of your life.

By now, you've seen that implementing the process of great leadership is hard. It requires consistent and focused humility and discipline. Even with this humility and discipline in place, we stumble. There always seems to be something lurking around the corner that is trying to derail our ability to accomplish something bigger than ourselves.

In the final element of the leadership process, we're going to look at that "something" that works doggedly to subvert our leadership efforts and, for that matter, our efforts to become better human beings. That something is the "Resistance."[74] Its definition is, "The refusal to accept or comply with something; the attempt to prevent something by Action or argument."

---

74 Dispenza, Dr. Joe. *You Are the Placebo: Making Your Mind Matter*. 2nd ed. Carlsbad, CA: Hay House, 2014.

For our purposes, we'll further define the "Resistance" as that unexplained force of nature that works to stop you from accomplishing something bigger than yourself. This is what leadership is—something bigger than yourself.

For example, the Resistance does not show itself when you are happily eating greasy takeout food on the couch while you binge-watch the latest iteration of junk TV. The Resistance feeds that behavior.

But you will find the Resistance sitting on the same couch, but this time, you're deciding to watch an educational documentary and eat non-processed, heart-healthy organic food. When you begin trying to make positive changes in your life, you can always count on the Resistance showing itself.

What's another example? Well, the Resistance won't show itself when you are firmly planted inside a group of people and participating in bad-mouthing or gossiping about someone else. And, of course, that someone is not in earshot. The Resistance feeds that behavior.

But, you are likely to come across the Resistance if inside that same group of people, you don't participate in the bad-mouthing or gossip. Even more antagonizing toward the Resistance, you walk away or speak out against this abhorrent behavior. The Resistance cannot tolerate that behavior and will make a strong showing either within yourself, everywhere else, or both. Because that's where the Resistance lives, within yourself and everywhere else.

The Resistance will take many forms when it shows itself: uncertainty, fear, ego, jealousy, anger, procrastination, judgment, self-doubt, or laziness. The number of ways the Resistance can take hold seems endless.

The leadership process is common sense so it's hard to reject the validity of the process. It makes a positive impact on the individual and collectively as it calls for people to raise their level of consciousness as teams, leaders, and human beings. Yet, despite its common sense and effectiveness, people will resist it. You will resist it at times. Why? Because it calls for higher awareness, reflection, and positive Action—the very things the Resistance refuses to tolerate.

As long as you are trying to achieve excellence, the Resistance will never go away. The Resistance is an ongoing Contingency that you, the leader, should always expect and account for. We know that people are going to naturally resist something that is unfamiliar to them because they have already neurochemically conditioned themselves to a particular behavior based on past emotions they keep reliving.[75]

So, when you begin to implement Guidelines for Behavior or SMACCC, it will be unfamiliar to your people. They will resist. What does this knowledge do for us as leaders? It gives us awareness, so we don't need to take the inevitable resistance personally because it's very likely not personal. It's a neurochemical addiction.

---

75   Pressfield, Steven. *The War of Art : Break Through the Blocks and Win Your Inner Creative Battles.* 1st ed. North Egremont, MA: Black Irish Entertainment LLC, 2002.

When the Resistance Hits the Team

It's one thing to combat the Resistance using the leadership process for our own inner demons. But what about when the Resistance infiltrates your team? What then? It's the same answer: go back to the process.

When a member or members of your team are hit with the Resistance, you'll feel something; you'll have an emotion. You'll recognize something isn't right. Maybe in this instance, you are feeling insecure or unsure of yourself as a leader because your plan or overall process is facing Resistance. Simply paint by numbers: identify your emotions, go through TRIGGER to EMOTION to THINK/DECIDE to ACTION. Inside of THINK and DECIDE, employ SMACCC and review if what you are doing is consistent with the team's Guidelines for Behavior.

When the Resistance hits your team, as it inevitably will, check yourself first inside all the elements of the leadership process. If you missed something the process will tell you and you can make the adjustments. If you haven't missed anything, it will be time for the next step. But for now, check yourself. Here's what your internal SMACCC dialogue might look like:

- Situation: The Resistance is speaking to my team in "this" way.

- Mission: Ensure the directions you provided to the team are clear, fair, and reasonable. Have you followed the leadership process and made clear what everyone will be held accountable for?

- Actions:
  - Review the Guidelines for Behavior. Have you made clear what behaviors your team will be held accountable for?
  - Have you consistently reviewed the Guidelines for Behavior regularly, and are you having people answer for them when they are not followed?
  - Review the plan for the current initiative and ensure you have accounted for all the elements of SMACCC.
  - Review your recent Actions. Have they been driven by emotions, or have you been making conscious decisions based on your emotions?

- Contingencies:
  - You find some holes in the plan because you missed an element of SMACCC or never clearly identified a behavior you were expecting from everyone. Good! Now you know the Resistance is likely coming from an unclear plan or behavioral guideline, so the team is acting out of sorts. You'll make the proper adjustments, Communicate them to the team, and move forward.
  - You make the adjustments, and the Resistance persists. That's OK because you've checked SMACCC and covered all the elements. The plan is solid. You've reiterated your behavioral guidelines and ensured everyone was clear on them and in agreement. Now you must be patient and courageous and trust the process. It's just the Resistance talking to your team. But, you always account for the Resistance as a running Contingency,

and you know the process can beat the Resistance. So, you press on unemotionally and methodically.

- Command: You are in Command! You are the leader, and you are in charge of your decisions and Actions ... not the fear and chaos the Resistance is trying to create.

- Communication: How will you communicate with the team? With consistency and confidence because you know you have put the right thought into your decisions and Actions because you have covered all the elements of the process.

We use SMACCC to fight the Resistance toward the process.

Now everything should be alright, right? Well, I hate to break it to you, but despite your best efforts, some of your people may lose the battle with the Resistance. So now what do you do?

Moving from Accountability to Consequence

This is where we move from accountability to consequence. Remember, accountability is not a bad word. It's simply asking someone to account for their Actions. It doesn't matter if the answer is good, bad, or somewhere in the middle. If you've asked the question and received an answer, you've held someone accountable. And, if you've followed the elements of the process, then you will have made clear WHAT people are being held accountable for.

Likewise, if you've made clear what people are being held accountable for, you've also reiterated these expectations on a consistent basis. Let's break this accountability-to-consequence thing down from the beginning as it relates to your people losing the battle to the Resistance.

You've worked the leadership process. You've become situationally aware of emotions and what your team does by practicing Emotional and Cultural Awareness and Recognition. Since you're now fully aware and in tune with your surroundings, you are able to identify Guidelines for Behavior that will define your culture and make you and your team better.

You also know that for the Guidelines for Behavior to stick, you must reiterate them consistently and on a regular basis, so your team is aware of their importance. There is no question at this point that your Guidelines for Behavior are how your team does business.

You are also conscious that for projects to succeed, it is critical to follow the elements of SMACCC. By following the elements of SMACCC and making your team aware that they will be held accountable for these elements of the Planning Process, you've added another layer of clarity regarding their accountability.

As you battle small bouts of Resistance through the process, which is normal, you go about the business of making small corrections where necessary. You can easily do this because people are fully aware of what they are being held accountable for, and a simple reminder of "that's not how we do business here" is all that's required to keep the momentum going. Because the Resistance is a running Contingency for you, you are always on the lookout for it and ready to battle it unemotionally and methodically.

In short, when there is a misstep, you don't go directly to consequence. You go to accountability first by asking them to explain their Actions and refocusing them on what they are being held accountable for. Because the environment you've created is clear and predictable, and everyone is speaking the same leadership language, people like coming to work, and the team morale is high.

However, there's always that one person who is not responding to proper accountability. So, like a good leader, you've checked your process to ensure that this one person's Resistance is not because of a misstep you've made. You ensure that this person's roles and responsibilities inside of the plans they have been a part of have been clear. You've ensured you've held them accountable by asking them "why?" when they haven't done what's been assigned or asked of them. When they continue to ignore the Guidelines for Behavior, you ensure you have made them clear to this person and that they have been communicated to on a regular basis.

You've checked your process every time your problem employee has gone off track. You've tried to make positive corrections each time, to no avail. The Resistance has gotten the best of your employee on a regular basis. Your efforts to affect positive change in your employee through the leadership process have failed.

Here's where the shift takes place. At some point, as this poor behavior continues, the fault moves from the employee to you, the leader. Why? Because people will continue to exhibit the behavior that is tolerated. If you tolerate a behavior, what you say about the behavior will no longer matter. This is when we move from accountability to consequence.

When this happens, following the leadership process gives you the justification to implement consequence, which is an unfortunate but real aspect of leadership. And consequence can mean many things.

Initially, the consequences were simply being held accountable by having to explain their conduct. Everybody goes through this at one point or another, so it's not a big deal. But as the poor behavior continues, the consequences need to become more real and can move to being moved off a project, demoted, or worst of all, terminated.

The point is, because you have followed the process for accountability, you've already done the necessary work to justify the consequences you impose. It's simply a by-product of following a tried-and-true leadership process, and the decision to move to consequence speaks for itself. This is how a leader determines if someone is not a cultural fit for your organization.

Work the Resistance

At this point, you've worked hard at having complete situational awareness at all times. Use your newfound awareness of all things to spot the Resistance and account for it. As with every other challenge you face, when you catch it early enough, you will be able to make small, easy adjustments before things get out of hand.

A Final Note

I T IS MY SINCERE HOPE THAT YOU TRULY MAKE THE ICE COLD Leader Methodology your own to create massive impact on your life and the lives of those around you. There is nothing more important than leadership in this world. I believe that with every fiber of my being.

When there is no love, a leader will recognize it, find out why, and move people toward love. When there is no patience, a leader will exercise patience in the face of impatience and change the energy of everyone they come in contact with. Leaders move intolerance to tolerance, worthlessness to worthiness, despair to hope, ignorance to understanding, and sadness to joy.

You can do all of these things. We all can, but only if we work at it—only if we care enough to go through the pain of growth in all the aspects of leadership we have discussed throughout this book.

It won't be easy. It will take discipline and humility that is uncommon to the uncommitted. It will take a new mindset. But now, you know how to achieve that new mindset. It will take practice to figure out exactly what works for you.

But now, you know how to practice. You know SMACCC. You know cold exposure. You can reflect back and see where you went right and where you went wrong. And now, you have that process and its five elements.

As my favorite quote in the world goes, "God will not look you over for medals, degrees, or diplomas, but for scars." Welcome to leadership!

Acknowledgments

NOTHING WORTH ITS SALT GETS DONE ALONE. MY JOURNEY, my recovery, and this book are no exception. Without the strength, patience, love, and friendship of my wife my journey ends in a crash landing, recovery does not happen, and this book is not written. Thank you, Jen. You are the true love and light of my life.

Thanks to my friend and former Navy SEAL Commander Mark Divine, who was the first person to open my eyes to the effects of traumatic brain injury and opened my mind to the fact that maybe, just maybe, I had an injury. And that it was the injury to my brain that was the source of my pain, not some random personality defect. This truly set me on a new path toward recovery. Thank you, Mark.

Encouragement is great, but it generally fades. Unless that encouragement is coming from David Amerland, who from the inception of *Ice Cold Leader* has consistently been there to offer guidance, opinions, and, of course, encouragement. Thank you, David, for your role as a true mentor and friend.

No amount of success comes unless we find people who are at the level we want to be. Thankfully, we found those people. Thank you, Darami Coulter, for sharing your friendship, knowledge, sense of humor, A-list wisdom, and most important your sympathetic ear. Thank you, Alyssa Fechner, for the same, as well as appreciating and welcoming "Raw Errol" to our discussions. Thank you, Daniel Decker, for taking a chance on us. Without you, this does not happen.

Thank you, Dr. John Hughes. You were there to speak to me about my struggles before I knew why I struggled. You went out of your way to get me to your office to conduct a brain scan, which showed the severity of my TBI. And then you asked questions. You asked about me. You asked about my leadership process. You asked about my wellness practices. And then, you put it all together for me. You explained how I saved my own life. And after I initially rejected the idea of treatment, you asked me one simple question that changed my life, "Wouldn't you like to feel better?" Thank you, Dr. John Hughes, for saving my life.

Thank you, Jessie Jay, for your photographic artistry, support, and friendship. Thank you, Sara Stibitz, for your incredible work and expertise not once, but twice.

And last but certainly not least, to Katie and Sheldon, thank you.

The list of people I can thank for the creation of this book seems endless because it is. For people who have supported me during my darkest days over the years I thank you. You didn't know why I went to dark places, you just knew that sometimes I went there. You never questioned me. You just supported me. I owe you all everything.

Find Out More About
Ice Cold Leader

IF YOU'D LIKE TO CONTINUE THE CONVERSATION ABOUT HOW to become an Ice Cold Leader, upcoming events, or how to bring Errol in for speaking, workshops, or training, contact us here:

Email: Hello@Icecoldleader.com

Instagram: https://www.instagram.com/the_ice_cold_leader/

LinkedIn: https://www.linkedin.com/in/errol-doebler/

Facebook: https://www.facebook.com/icecoldleader

Errol and *Ice Cold Leader* deliver their one-of-a-kind message of leadership and personal excellence through process and wellness in several different ways.

- To learn more about the course, go to https://icecold leader.com/the-course/

- To learn more about the coaching, go to https://icecold leader.com/coaching/

- To learn more about the events, go to https://icecoldlead er.com/ice-cold-leader-events/

- To learn more about keynote speaking, go to https://ice coldleader.com/keynote/